# John Lennon 4 Ever

by
Conrad Snell
Special Writing Consultant
Howard M. Morgan

Copyright © 1981 by Crown Summit Books
ISBN: 0-939184-00-1

Cover Illustration and Design by
Michael Macias Design Studio

All rights reserved, which includes the right to reproduce this book or portions thereof in any form whatsoever.

First Crown Summit Printing, January, 1981

Printed in the U.S.A.

# Contents

| | | |
|---|---|---|
| 1 | The One We Loved | 1 |
| 2 | Elvis Inspired John | 11 |
| 3 | He Conquered America | 19 |
| 4 | Experimenting Words & Sounds | 29 |
| 5 | John As Film Star | 41 |
| 6 | Experimenting With Meditation | 49 |
| 7 | John and His Loves | 59 |
| 8 | The Downfall | 71 |
| 9 | Fight His Youth | 79 |
| 10 | Settling In | 87 |
| 11 | He Made Us Happy | 101 |
| Chronology of John Lennon 1940-1980 | | 107 |
| Sources | | 135 |

# 1

## The One We Loved

# 1

What fun it had been to come out into the open once again. Since the cutting of his and her new album "Double Fantasy," suddenly the world was once again talking frequently about the Lennons and what they were doing. There was no doubt about it. Yoko Ono was right when she mentioned to an interviewer that the president of the United States spoke for the people of the United States, but the Lennons had a much broader range, they spoke for the world.

He had said to someone in recent days that he was only 40, "God willing, there are another 40 years of productivity to go."

The Lennons had spent the past three hours talking about their works and their future. John and Yoko had sat in their seventh floor apartment answering questions from reporters assigned to the exclusive interview by RKO Radio Network.

One of the statements John made seemed full of optimism and hope, "While there's life, there's hope... We're going to live or we're going to die." Then he casually said, "If we're dead, we're going to have to deal with that, if we're alive we're going to have to deal with being alive. So worrying about whether Wall Street or the Apocalypse is going to come in the form of the great beast is not going to do us any good day today."

It was early evening. The Lennons had slowly descended in the gilded elevator from their apartment where they had lived for the past half decade to the street below. They were on their way to the Record Plant Studio on West 44th Street in New York City, the city John had grown to love. At the entrance to the nearly hundred-year-old apartment building, John stopped to sign a thrust out album cover of his latest release, "Double Fantasy." Perhaps John took no note of the moment.

After all, it was John who had not many weeks earlier told an interviewer how one faces life: "The unknown is what it is. And to be frightened of it is what sends everybody scurrying around chasing dreams, illusions, war, peace, love, hate, all that—it's all illusion." Then he summarized with, "Accept that it's unknown and it's plain sailing. Everything is unknown—then you're ahead of the game. That's what it is. Right...?"

It had been this way since the day the Lennons took up residence in the Victorian apartment complex across the street from Central Park. Fans would rush up with flowers, note pads, gifts, and strange objects as soon as John and Yoko would emerge from the entrance to the apartment building. It seemed the rock fans never tired of giving their adulation to one so loved.

Of course John was accustomed to the constant flow of people wanting to touch him or simply speak to him, or have his signature.

It had been thus seemingly forever. As soon as the doorman opened the doors, a half dozen people or more would come to life after waiting for hours to see their idol. As it usually happened, Yoko would continue on to open the door of their limosine while the hungry autograph seekers hounded her husband who had to fight off thrust out envelopes or gifts.

John loved people and since he was, in this era of his life, a peaceable man, he would sign the paper or album and even chat briefly to the listening flock.

Did he worry about his or Yoko's safety?

This kind of crowd adulation had been going on for over fifteen years. Certainly it was nothing new. Actually, he had become accustomed to it and saw it perhaps as a harmless nuisance—like a litter of pups pawing at his legs to get attention from the master. Once asked if he was concerned for his safety he replied, in an off-handed manner, "They don't mean any harm. They're just fans. They just want to let you know they care. Besides, what are you going to do? You can't spend all of your life hiding from people. You've got to get out and live some, don't you."

That evening a chubby young man, who had been standing outside the Dakota apartments and had stepped up with his album, had been waiting for hours. Actually, according to reports, he had planned to get the signature for weeks. He had traveled all the way from Hawaii for this special visit with John Lennon. A young photographer, who had stood with the chubby young man named Mark David Chapman, took a color shot of Lennon signing Chapman's album.

The Lennons sat snugly in their hired limousine as it pulled away from the curb bound for West 44th. Chapman then turned to his street acquaintance and showed the photographer John Lennon's scrawled signature "John Lennon 1980" across the cover.

"John Lennon signed my album," he declared to the photographer. "Nobody in Hawaii is going to believe me."

Both young men would wait another two hours for the Lennons to return before the photographer would declare he had stayed long enough in the December chill. Chapman would try to get him to stay by telling him that Lennon would be back soon and he too could get his autograph. The photographer begged off by declaring that he would return another time.

"I'd wait," Chapman advised, "You never know if you'll see him again."

At the record studio, the Lennons, with the help of a producer and sound technicians, mixed sounds on their new single titled, "Walking On Thin Ice." At 10:30 they left the studio, planning to go out to eat, then return, but instead they decided to return to the Dakota.

It was 10:50 p.m. when the limousine pulled up to the curb near the arch. The driver could have driven inside the grey-brown stone fronted archway to a driveway in the interior, but did not. Yoko and John alighted from the rear seat of the car. Both started up the driveway to the ironwork gate, Yoko walking a few feet ahead of her husband when they heard a voice from behind them shout "Mr. Lennon."

Lennon craned his neck to glance back at the voice when he must have seen the young man crouched just five feet away gripping the trigger of his .38 special with both hands. According to witnesses, Chapman pumped four rapid shots into Lennon's stunned body. Lennon looked incredulous as he weaved, struggling six steps before collapsing into the doorman's office.

Yoko, dressed in a fur coat, whirled about reaching to support her wounded husband. She held tightly to his head and shoulders as the blood drained from his slight body.

The gunman stood in place. The doorman kicked the gun away exclaiming, "Do you know what you did?" In a sort of daze he replied, "I just shot John Lennon."

John Lennon must have felt the burden of no father model. The skies rained down German bombs on the Liverpool seaport that October day in 1940 when John was born. Freddy, his father, had already left for sea months earlier, leaving John's mother, Julia, a giddy, irrational woman, to try and cope with motherhood alone. She failed miserably.

Years later John would meet his father. A London

newspaper, the Daily Express, ran a picture of the itinerant ship's steward reduced to washing dishes in a small hotel in London. By the time the embarrassing photo popped up in the Express, anyone who had not heard of John Lennon would have to have been locked in a cellar for the past five years. Famous and rich, John read the news story about how his father had granted an interview in the kitchen of the small hotel not far from the stock broker belt outside London. The father had already tried to contact his famous son by letter in an effort to create some type of father-son relationship. John, on the other hand, had refused to see the older man. After all, by that time he had totally abandoned John's mother and John had surmised in his youth that his father would suddenly appear once John had made it to the top. The newspaper article mentioned the fact that John rejected his father, so rather than continue on with bad press, John took his "blackmailing" father under his wing and supported him until he died several years later of cancer.

The mother of John Lennon took a strange position regarding her son. She was the youngest of five sisters, and with the vanishing of John's father, she wearied of the role of mother and provider. So she talked her older sister, Mimi, and her husband, George, a dairy farmer, into taking John at age 4 to raise him.

When John was 16, his mother, who had experienced difficulty in coping with life, was struck down and killed by a drunk off-duty police officer as she stood on a street curb awaiting a bus. John mentioned to an interviewer, later, how he lost his mother twice: first when he moved in with his Auntie and second when she died. Just prior to her death, their contacts had become more and more frequent. He had become old enough to begin to know his mother and begin the process of trying to understand why she had not raised him. Both parents had left a void in the young man's early development but more especially his mother. When Julia died, according to John's first wife Cynthia, "John was left full of emptiness and bitterness, and the hard exterior he built was self-protective. He didn't want to be hurt anymore." The name Julia would pop up in years to come in naming his son Julian and in numerous ways in John's music.

Contrary to all the press about John being raised in the slums of Liverpool, his aunt and uncle owned a small, comfortable home in one of the better middle-class neighborhoods of Liverpool, not more than a fifteen minute walk from John's mother's place. It was the auntie who reared John with English strictness and no nonsense behavior. The task was never easy.

John entered Quarry Bank Grammar where the Latin motto and uniforms must have early on cramped his easy-going, never conform attitude. His schooling was a continuous rampage of disruption and pranks. Such things as gambling on the school field or dumping trash and dusters out of the second story school windows, or simply not attending class were but a few of the non-conformist behavior he displayed on a regular basis. It was always the auntie who had to face the rigors of raising an incorrigible nephew. There seemed to be no encouragement that Mimi could invent to lift John from the failure status that the school masters had tagged to John Winston Lennon—though, in fact, he was perhaps the brightest student in school.

Outside school he was as much the hellraiser as inside. His influence on other youths ranged far and wide in the neighborhood. If any vandalism were reported to the local constable, it was likely John had participated in the crime.

He loved his auntie but refused to conform to standard conduct. Even he later referred to those years as ones where he had a chip on his shoulder. He mentioned that his attitude caused parents of his teen-age friends to shun him and demanded that their children do the same.

Actually, John grew up knowing he had family and that on the ladder of British economic status he was a rung above the boys in the street. His uncle provided for the family a comfortable suburban home where John felt accepted. He went from high school to college with the kindly help of a liberal school master who recommended him to the college.

Out of the experience of those years of growing up in Liverpool came many future songs, but one that expressed an exact spot of John's youth was "Strawberry Fields Forever." Near the semi-detached house of his aunt and uncle was pleasant, a reformatory for boys. It sported gardens called Strawberry Fields. There John attended garden parties with his friends, Nigel and Pete. The three generally went to sell lemonade bottles. Strawberry Fields remained a pleasant memory for an otherwise troubled youth.

John viewed himself as brighter and more creative than other children. As early as kindergarten he was always what he called "hip." Even though he had deep insecurities and was not expecially outgoing, in his mind he was "hip." Very early in his youth John identified with the legendary Lewis Carroll. Years later when a drug generation would refer to John's music, "Lucy In The Sky With Diamonds," as the cover for LSD, he denied it was so.

He fantasized with the Lewis Carroll characters. He insisted that the words of some of his lyrics came from "Alice In Wonderland." He had Alice in a boat buying an egg that became Humpty Dumpty. The "Kaleidoscope eyes" of Lucy came from that same imagery John had adopted from Carroll, whom he must have admired. He pulled other images from Carroll. When John wrote "I Am A Walrus," it too came from Alice in wonderland in the segment of "The Walrus and the Carpenter."

In those developing years John saw things differently than those about him. He could look in the bathroom mirror and see his image twisted and changed. Things seemed to be going on in his head that no one else experienced, or if they did they never mentioned it to John.

Newsweek said of John Lennon, "He was an impudent lower-middle-class kid who from an early age had a sense of balked power. 'When I was about 12,' he said, 'I used to think I must be a genius but nobody's noticed.'"

Before her death, during that "getting acquainted" period with his mother, Julia taught John guitar. She had skill with a banjo and coupled that with humorous songs. Actually, John saw enough of his mother before her death to gain insights into her personality that freed him to express a sense of humor. Sometimes she would "go for a walk with him wearing a pair of panties on her head and sporting spectacles without lenses through which she'd scratch her eyes to disconcert passers-by."

He would mourn the death of such a free spirit throughout the remainder of his exciting life.

# 2

*Elvis Inspired John*

# 2

At the age of 16, John basked in the sensational new rock and roll sounds coming out of America. The music touched him like no influence before. He was eager to know everything about the uproarious American, Elvis Presley. Up to that time nothing had so riveted his total senses as did the palpitating sounds of Elvis singing such hits as "You Ain't Nothing But A Hound Dog" or "Heartbreak Hotel." John squeezed in wherever he could get a view of Elvis on the telly.

He begged and cajoled his auntie into buying him a cheap Spanish guitar, then he cast around for a group to join or create.

Suddenly his main goal in life was to be as big as Elvis. "At the time," one observer stated, "he was thinking merely of the rewards of rock stardom: the fame, the money and the excitement." Ironically, in years to come at the death of Elvis, John's reaction by the press to the American tragedy was sought far and wide, but John that year was secluded in the mountains of Japan. If he hadn't been, he very well may have broken his self-imposed silence to utter public statements on his affection for Presley.

At times John would long for the thrill of America. He would leave his auntie's home and ride to Pier Head and while gazing out at the wide Mersey River he knew in his heart that one day he would live in America, the land of his great affections where Elvis had opened the wide door to rock, a door that John would step through to make an impact on the wild explosive music that would never be forgotten.

John spearheaded the formation of the skiffle group. He pulled together friends from Quarry Bank and a neighboring school called Liverpool Institute Grammar School. As the leader of the newly formed Quarry Men band, John got the group into school socials, neighborhood parties and church socials. During the summer of 1957 an interesting association developed at Woolton Parish Church where John met 16-year-old Liverpool Institute student, Paul McCartney. The Quarry Men were playing a social and with some detachment John struck up a relationship with McCartney. They found mutual thrills listening to Elvis and Chuck Berry strum their special brand of rock and roll on records.

Paul was nothing like John. He had come out of a government housing district of Allerton where he had been raised in a strict conservative environment. He had a handsomeness that lent itself to a calm, pleasing personality and which would immediately dub him diplomat of the group as he joined in with the band. Paul once noted that John played the guitar like a banjo and seemed to have knowledge of any form of music.

John never concerned himself with form or even lyrics to a song. If he didn't know them he made up his own words, tossing them in like bits of stone in a cement mix. With his reckless need to make music, any kind of music, and his low level of conventionality, he inserted words in song from whatever popped into his head. The band drew heavily upon established American sounds, where rhythm and blues lifted from generations of blacks who had already given the sound soul.

John's interests ranged wide when he wasn't playing in his band. He entered Liverpool Art College and found immediate success in drawing and painting, though music still dominated his creative thinking. It was about that time that the tag-along kid, George Harrison, joined in the band.

There was little financial success to keep members of the band tightly knit. Members came and went, but somehow John, Paul and George stayed on to beat out the sounds with cheap guitars, tea-chest basses and washboards. Fortunately, Allan Williams, a struggling coffee house owner offered his services as the band's manager. He in some strange manner gave the group a professional status, and even found them work in and out of the country. Through Williams' influence they wangled a stint in Hamburg, Germany in 1960. About that time Williams gave up on the group and wiped them from his life.

The little joint in Germany called Indra was in the sleazy red light district of an industrial port city, but it was here that the band did things to create a sensational mood. John twisted and screamed and even out-Elvised Elvis. Things took a turn for the worst when George Harrison was deported because he was under age. Then to top it off, the group's pad caught fire one day.

But the stint in Germany paid off. They returned twice over a period of eighteen months and got jobs in other clubs in Hamburg. On one of those visits home, they landed a slot at the Cavern Club in Liverpool. By that time, they were calling themselves the Silver Beatles. At first someone suggested they be the b-e-e-t-l-e-s, then John, quick to bastardize words, thought of "beat" as in rock and roll sounds, thus the spelling of the bug changed to B-E-A-T-L-E-S.

The Cavern Club was nothing more than a rundown, ill-kept cellar situated under a warehouse on Matthew Street in Liverpool. It was a joint doomed to be destroyed one day by city developers. In 1980 it would become a parking lot and reverent fans of John Lennon's would search out what they sensed to be the exact spot under the pavement where the struggling Beatles had performed in the early '60s.

The band played noon and night at the Cavern. It was excellent training with sound and form. There evolved a cadence and flair to the Beatle's music that began to draw a following. It became fashionable for all types of people to frequent the Cavern Club to hear the sounds of the local band that some still called the Silver Beatles. Williams' void left the group open to most anyone with an idea and connections in the music business. The managerial voice soon was filled by a stroke of luck that seemed to always occur just as the group needed help. Brian Epstein dropped in to hear the music of the group that some of his customers had been asking about in his record store.

Epstein's conservative Jewish background gave the band the kind of managerial class it needed to spread the sound. Brian was older, 27, but not so old that he was out of touch with the sounds and feelings of youth. Brian liked Lennon from the start and the others simply came as part of the package he hoped to promote.

Actually, Epstein had no background or training in the field of promoting a musical group. He had been part of his family's retail trade business with his task, running a record store. He took on the challenge of managing the Beatles as a step up in his life.

His first order of business with the rock and roll group was the group itself. He was a stickler for detail. He groomed them in suits and a unique hair style that resembled the innocence and charm of a little Lord Fauntleroy. It was a look totally foreign to John, who naturally protested all the while, but nevertheless, dressed up while trying to decide whether to return to art or play the role and see where it would lead him. He stayed on. It seems certain that John reluctantly consented to the demands of Brian, realizing that he would have his day. One thing Brian could not achieve was harnessing John's mouth. Like his mother before him, John said whatever he pleased and cared not one whit what anyone thought of it. To the dismay of Epstein, John would blurt out the most obscene and, at times, meaningless comments he had ever heard.

It's thought by many that if Brian Epstein had not stepped into the Cavern that day, there would likely have never been world adulation of the Beatles. Brian's life was not at all compatible with the Beatles. He came from a Jewish trade family, conservative, proper and not at all used to the wild antics of the Beatles, yet he accepted the role of manager and flung all his considerable energies into the task that led him uptown to a host of recording companies. Each record company had its own reasons for rejecting something so unorthodox as the Beatles' rock and roll sound. Only in the confines of searching out *anyone* who recorded professionally, did Brian come across A & R. It was run by a congenial fellow named George Martin. He ended up offering the Beatles their first record contract by paying them a penny a record royalties.

The Beatles recorded "Love Me Do," and made it to an astonishing 17th place on the British records top 20. They cut a second, "Please, Please me." It climbed to number 1 in all Britain by March of 1963. In the process of recording the above two titles, the group lost a drummer and gained a young "cute" fellow named Starkey, who used the show name of Ringo Starr. He must have been especially ordered because from there on out the hits kept coming.

In the first flush of popularity, with teenage girls screaming and scheming to touch them, the Beatles hit stardom like nothing the world had ever seen. John read how Elvis had made 100 million dollars in his first two years on top of the hits, how he had a jet plane, Cadillacs, a Rolls-Royce and all the trappings of stardom. It may not have, at that time, dawned on John that Elvis was also snagged by his popularity into becoming a house prisoner—no longer could he venture into the streets, or even go down to the casino in whichever super hotel he happened to be playing in Las Vegas. Wherever he went, fans swarmed.

The status of being a superstar became clear to John when the teenage girls of London swept over the Beatles in such frenetic screaming and clawing that wherever they went, hordes of fans followed. The Daily Mirror dubbed the hysteria, "Beatlemania."

The madness for anything of the Beatles swept far beyond England. America and the entire western world was caught up in the fever. Someone also labeled them the Fab Four.

# 3

*He Conquered America*

# 3

According to the book, *Beatles In Their Own Words* John Lennon hungered for the conquest of America in 1964. That tour represented the height he sought. Since Elvis first set John's desires aflame, he had one goal, to be greater than Elvis. "I knew all about Johnnie Ray and Frankie Laine and Tennessee Ernie Ford," John was quoted in the *Globe* as saying, "But my mother heard one of the early Presley records and told me he was like all of three of them rolled into one. I listened to the record and went out of my mind. After that we all tried to be like Elvis."

John realized that there was just one Elvis. Elvis had the superstar image even into the 60s and yet all the star from memphis could really do was strum the guitar and use his voice and body. John had that and much more. John had the mind of a composer. Still in all, to break through the overpowering forces of popularity that Elvis had garnered, John would have to be part of a group. In John's mind, since the Beatles was his own creation and he was the heart and soul and mind of that group, if the group's fame were greater than Elvis' singly, then it would actually be for all intents and purposes, John Lennon the greatest.

Said John of that moment in his rise to international superstardom, "You see we wanted to be bigger than Elvis—that was the main thing. We reckoned we could make it because there were four of us. None of us would've made it alone, because Paul was not quite strong enough, I didn't have enough girl appeal. George was too quiet and Ringo was the drummer. But we thought that everyone would be able to dig at least one of us..."

John's hunch was right. They stormed the very gates of America forcing Elvis to share the light.

The conquest of America began with groundwork laid by their dedicated manager Brian Epstein. There is no question in the minds of serious students of the Beatle's rise to international fame, that without Epstein, the Beatles would have ended their music in the Cavern at Liverpool. Epstein had a passion to make the Beatles great. He loved them. He was like a big brother who had a tingling feeling for the worth of their talent.

Epstein had one other asset that set him apart from the norm—he had great charm and skill in tight negotiations with the leading power-brokers in music.

Epstein made certain that the Beatle's music got top billing in every rock and roll radio station in America, thus to insure a sellout crowd when the Beatles consented to come. The teenagers of America cooperated by listening to and buying such hits as "Love Me Do," "Please, Please Me," and "From Me to You." The kids loved the new sound of the Liverpool four.

Ed Sullivan, America's most popular T.V. variety show host, saw the Beatles at the airport in London when his plane awaited departure. He stood dumbfounded at the teenage airport response to the incoming flight of the Beatles. He met them on the spot and signed them to an appearance on his Sunday night show.

It was a great time to keep the Beatles under wraps until the right moment came to introduce them to America.

## He Conquered America

Billboard Magazine listed the Beatle's fourth single, "I Want To Hold Your Hand," as the number one record. This opened the doors for wild excitement.

Epstein flew to New York to lay the right plans for that invasion. Since Ed Sullivan had already signed to have the Beatles on his show, and the plans were in effect to give the Beatles T.V. exposure, Epstein needed to garner other sources of publicity. The radio was possible, but perhaps too overused for what he wished to attempt.

The New York Times quoted Ed Sullivan's experience in London at the time the Beatles returned to London from Stockholm where they had been in concert, "I made up my mind that this was the same sort of mass hit hysteria that had characterized the Elvis Presley days." Ed was the type of showman who looked for something big. He longed to scoop the entertainment field as a talent scout of the first order and he always sought an exclusive on his show.

Epstein by-passed radio. It was far too expensive and purely commercial. The press, on the other hand, was not a paid announcement. If newspeople saw a story and published it in the normal channels of reporting, people took it seriously. In two major interviews, Epstein got coverage. *The New York Times* and *The New Yorker*, each published significant articles on the coming of the Beatles to New York. From those two stories, the wire services picked up tidbits that they scattered across the country.

Capitol records had not seen the potential in their contract with the Beatles until January 1964 when the release of "I Want To Hold Your Hand" reached number one in America, February 1st. Capitol records had earlier bought their recording contract. They put up $50,000 in publicity funds to enhance their investment. They also sank the money into retaining 16 press agents who went to work creating teenage hysteria at the arrival of the Beatles, who were set to appear on Ed Sullivan's show in February.

"The Beatles Are Coming" posters appeared across America, but particularly in New York where the Fab Four were scheduled to land. The landing was a smash hit that evening T.V. news picked up and broadcast everywhere. Some said there were as many as 10,000 fans on hand at the airport in New York City. Actually, it was more like half that number, still in all, no one had seen anything like it for pop music stars.

One of the causes for the huge turnout was radio. New York's pop music stations shouted out periodic bulletins on the Beatles' flight arrival. That simply fueled the flames of teenage eagerness to be on hand at the exciting happening.

It was more than the press agents had expected when the Beatles disembarked from their plane. Mostly girls screamed their lungs out. A makeshift press conference ensued allowing the Beatles to express their wit and charm.

Whereas news conferences with past stars from Hollywood or Memphis had been little more than nods for answers from the superstars, the Beatles set a new pattern of interviews. They never took themselves seriously so in those molding moments of Beatlemania at the airport, their comments were such that no one could pin them down.

One reporter shouted, "How do you account for your success?"

"We have a press agent," John shot back.

"Do you have a message for America?"

Paul responded with, "Yes, we do, actually ... buy more Beatles' records."

Their easy manner caught on from the start of their American conquest. Some writers have tagged the press as being impressed and taken offguard by the Beatles. That is doubtful. Most press people made no distinction between the four young men; they even confused their indentity. The New York Herald Tribune reported that the Beatles were, "slight kids from Liverpool who wear four-button coats, stove-pipe pants, ankle-high boots with Cuban heels and drool looks on their faces."

There was no publication devoted exclusively to rock and roll. The rising generation of pop journalists were just beginning to surface, thus there was little in the way of musical interpretation in the news. According to Geoffrey Stokes in his book on the Beatles, *The Beatles Some Years in the Life*, he mentioned that the "press coverage of the Beatles was almost universally favorable, it was, as it had been in England, focused on the event far more than on the music."

The Ed Sullivan show brought hordes of shrieking girls into that tiny studio theatre. The event had every teenager who cared to be in touch with the mood of the moment watching across the nation. Some reported the audience greater than the Kennedy and Nixon debates of 1960. Someone tabulated crime that hour in America and discovered there were no teenage arrests during the broadcast. There the four stood as Ed Sullivan plead for silence in the theatre, a silence he never got from the screaming girls in the audience. When the T.V. camera panned the group, according to one viewer, girls faces were "twisted in a melange of agony, ecstasy and despair."

That same viewer, a Mother, commenting in *Counsel*, told of her first Beatle impact. She said she had gone upstairs to her daughter's room to quiet her and her two frollicking friends, who were watching the Ed Sullivan show, "Judy was rolling on the bed, moaning; Melanie was on the floor, chewing a pillow; and my own grave Joanie, her mouth stuffed with her knuckles, looked like Hamlet seeing his father's ghost."

The Beatles were a smash hit. They reappeared on Ed's show in April of that year. In the interim, the Beatles assumed first, second, third, fourth and fifth positions on Billboard's singles charts. "Meet the Beatles," a Capitol release of the earlier "With the Beatles," hit the very top, destroying all LP record sales in the history of the industry.

On their third tour of the U.S. the Beatles captured a nation with their appearance at Shea's Stadium before 60,000 fans. They had such crazy lyrics as "You Say Yes, I Say No. You say stop, I say go. You say good-bye and I say hello."

Those tours kept the group cohesive. John and Paul sat

together throughout the period and wrote the lyrics that set the tone for their success. As long as they were together they wrote. Paul liked the softer, more wistful sounds and words of "The Long and Winding Road," and "Across the Universe." John's were harsher and in many ways more personal. And, too, they revealed his character. That undoubtedly was a key to his success as the leader of the organization.

The Beatles were off and running to make the pop history of the 1960s their very own. Elvis became keenly aware of just who the Beatles were. They had outsold the King.

The Beatles' second tour to the United States in the summer of 1964 threw the whole teenage population into a mad spin of excitement. They went first to Atlantic City where bedlam broke loose, forcing the tour to halt in hiding for a few days before attempting a bus trip up the Pike to a September concert in the Philadelphia Civic Center.

Phil Jansner, a disc jockey, remembered that Beatle visit to Philadelphia. That concert was the first time Phil had seen tickets sell out in 13 minutes flat and then watch scalpers go to work on blocks of seats. He mentioned how the police escort of the buses from Atlantic City to Philadelphia were decoys. The real Beatles arrived by "Hackey fish truck" to avoid the groupies that stormed the escorted buses.

That same tour wound its way to Las Vegas where the crowds at the convention center went wild. John had wanted to visit Las Vegas, the show capital, since he was first into music. But the concert may as well have been in Liverpool for all the view of Las Vegas he got.

At Las Vegas they had to drive from the airport on back roads to their Sahara Hotel room on the 19th floor. It seemed that all of Las Vegas was struck with Beatlemania. When they stopped at the hotel, three dozen teenage girls threw themselves across the hood of the car. When the Beatles emerged from the rear seats, girls leaped on them, tore at their clothes in a frenzy seldom, if ever, displayed in Las Vegas where the stars had descended for decades. That hot, summer night was unusual.

The other unusual happening for Las Vegas came during the two whirlwind performances. The Convention Center was sold out. "About 16,000 fans paid $4 a ticket for a chance to see—but not hear—the beatles. About 135 security guards ringed the stage to keep the fans from crushing the group." One promoter stood ten feet from the stage and claimed he couldn't hear the music because the screaming reverberated from 14,000 teenage girls who seemed not to take a breath." One young girl scratched her face raw as she watched her idols perform on stage..." There were even some of the more daring who rushed down the aisles and tried to hurtle themselves over the guards like flying quarterbacks.

Las Vegas rippled for days in the aftermath of the Beatles. The Sahara lost sheets, towels, blankets, lamps, anything and everything that the Beatles had touched. Rene Germanier outfoxed the security guard at the Sahara. The clever writer and photographer jumped on the service elevator and rode it to the 18th floor. He then jammed the double doors open with a free-standing ash tray and informed the security guard at the Beatles' door that the hotel manager had sent him to take shots of the Fab Four. He got in.

And the Beatles got out of Las Vegas without once seeing the famous strip John so longed to see. At least he was at last in America, even though he was not allowed to see because of poor crowd control.

They came back each season. They loved America and America loved them, though neither took the other seriously. On their second tour, the Beatles let it be known that they never claimed to be great musical talent, rather a sort of mopheaded, no-talent stage show of sounds. They really didn't need the sounds on stage because the shrieking of teenage girls drowned out all sound anyway.

Said Newsweek of the Beatles when they made their second tour of America, "Visually they are a nightmare: tight, dandified, Edwardian—Beatnik suits and great pudding bowls of hair. Musically they are a near-disaster:

guitars and drums slamming out a merciless beat that does away with secondary rhythms, harmony, and melody. Their lyrics (punctuated by hutty shouts of 'yeah, yeah, yeah!') are a catastrophe, a preposterous farrage of Valentine-card romantic sentiments. 'We're rather crummy musicians,' says George, the one who looks like a poet. 'We can't sing: we can't do anything,' adds Paul, the cherub. 'But we're having a great laugh."

For the next six years the hits came. From their light-hearted, fun-loving methods of stage madness to a year-by-year maturing, the fans grew up with them. The list of hits reads like glowing tickertape of successes.

A gold record was the big thing in those days. A gold meant the record made it past the million seller mark. Here are some of the outstanding solid gold records. Actually the Beatles won nearly half a hundred gold records. If anyone else in the pop music field were to win even a fourth of the amount the Beatles won in a decade, they would enjoy a prized position.

They achieved something that no other group in history had done—nearly fifty gold records which meant at least a million records for each title. In just a few short years they had grown from the simple, light strains of "I Want To Hold Your Hand" to the complex music of "Sgt. Pepper's Lonley Hearts Club Band." And in the process acquired not only fame and experience in sound, but a major fortune in revenues.

It was the fortune as much as anything that they never quite mastered. If it had not been for Epstein being there too, they may well have lost it. Though in all fairness to those around Brian Epstein, whose assignment it was to help corral and control the money, it took sharp, highly trained personnel to put the Beatle industry into manageable areas of profits and loss. It was mostly profit.

# 4

*Experimenting Words & Sounds*

# 4

When he wrote his evaluation of rock, Jeff Greenfield in the *New York Times* Magazine summed up the new trend of the '60s and especially the Beatles when he wrote about the young adults of that era being "more influential than ever before. And because the music had won acceptability, rock 'n roll was not judged indulgently as a 'boys will be boys' fad. Rock music was expressing a sensibility about the tangible world—about sensuality, about colors and sensations, about the need to change consciousness."

At the beginning of 1967 the Beatles released the "greatest single record of all times "—*Penny Lane* and *Strawberry Fields Forever.*"

The *New York Times* Magazine also mentioned how Lennon claimed that the "Beatles sometimes put elusive references into their songs just to confuse their more solemn interpreters." "I am the egg man," they sang, "not 'egghead.'"

The Beatles expanded rock and roll to a new and more elevated level of sound that became a standard for others to follow or imitate. All through their music it seemed impossible for others in the field to catch up. The music of John and Paul never remained static. It was not John's nature to do so. His very life was in constant change. From the start he set the pace with unconventional ways of doing things: playing his guitar like a banjo; his refusal to conform to established modes of singing, or the changing of lyrics to suit his taste, even when he was singing old Elvis numbers in the Cavern days.

It was Paul who mentioned that the Beatles would "stretch the limits of pop." They kept up a constant barrage of sound and innovative instruments to crash any conventional barrier. There may have been at least one other reason for their foray into the wilderness of rock; they never wanted to be thought of musically as someone's marionette. They were completely their own persons and proved it repeatedly.

They continued to have a wide scattering of staff people to guard their interests, but the Beatles made the final decisions. One of their decisions before the death of Epstein was to drop out of concerts and concentrate on recordings to forward their musical goals. This way, they could function musically without the constant melee of crowds. They wanted time to think through their music.

The critics said it couldn't be done. No group had ever stopped concerts and and buried themselves in the recording studio where the sounds were not spontaneous. They would soon fail. The Beatles were different. They broke all recording records without further live appearances.

Voices warned that "no one who had ever left the concert circuit to concentrate on merely recording had ever retained an audience." Those critics were unaware of the Beatles' new method of creating the recorded music. The Fab Four were not merely the type to sit around in some rehearsal hall pounding away at their music until they had just the right sound, then quickly call together all the musical talent and equipment they needed to record. Not at all. They began with the proper technical persons and equipment to help in the formation of the product. All four assumed a more professional level of recording by the time they dropped live performances to hide out in the studio. Of course, it was expensive and unheard of, but that was part of their innovation, along with enormous cash reserves.

In their formative years, they spent one day in the studio to cut "Please, Please Me." Not so with the new studio sound album titled "Sgt. Pepper's Lonely Hearts Club Band." They logged a full 700 hours spread over three months of studio time to complete that one album.

It is now a fact that the method they developed of dominating studio time to practice became standard for the industry when they achieved such resounding success using that technique.

They created rock's first concept album with "Sgt. Pepper." Cut on that hit were such pondering moods as "I read the news today oh boy," a bewildered statement of how troubled some were with the destructive forces at work in the world of 1967 or "A Day in the Life," a protest to those unleashed forces of political power, mainly eliminating from the most arrogant power as they saw it, the United States. It was true that what came out of those secluded, full-blown marathon studio sessions was the greatest contemporary music in the history of the art.

The Beatles' music changed the popular culture of the world. They had the rare ability to make their music overpoweringly appealing to the youth. It had, according to an article in *Time*, "eloquent melodies, pungent lyrics, and ingenious instrumental arrangements that mostly came from the heart and mind of Paul and John."

The mind and heart of John Lennon began to publicly surface long before the hysteria of Beatlemania softened from a roar to a rumble. People had already been alert to the lyrics of the music they hummed or mouthed and sought to know its composer.

Soon everyone discovered that there were basically two minds writing the pop-rock music which had wrapped itself around the ears of the world. The first cuts of "Please, Please

Me" and "I Want To Hold Your Hand" or "Can't Buy Me Love" were out and out heart throbbing, teenage toned love songs that certainly appealed to the girls at all the concerts. If the Beatles had continued with that brand of music, they likely would have remained secluded on their own English soil. One of the reasons that genre of music did not dominate their sound has to be the insistent John nudging his group to more vital issues. He truly never saw himself as a romantic idol, all clothed in the superstar popularity of an international singer, rather he was a creative force.

At this juncture, John, as well as Paul, divided off from most hit singers of the time. They persisted in doing something few other serious, popular entertainers ever did before—they wrote all their own material and it was obvious they felt the music because it had seeped and at times gushed out of their own minds and hearts. Elvis sang songs composed by others. John and Paul sang strictly their music. If the two Beatles were to be remembered for any outstanding talent, it was not voice or style alone, but also lyrics and poetry.

For the generation or two before the '60s, Rogers and Hammerstein, Lerner and Lowe were revered for their abilities to lift the hearts of the pop music lovers. It is a fact that Beatle John and Beatle Paul were intuitively in the same league with the pop music writers of the 20th century. Yet, John ranked with the greats of two centuries. His compositions were placed alongside the works of composers whose music has endured for decades and has given the world the stuff of symphonies: Muzak, Beethoven, Shubert and a host of others. For the late 20th century, the world will have to look to John Lennon among others for the music of this generation.

Though they were composers, neither John nor Paul read musical notes. They, of course, understood the lyrical sounds they combined into creative music, but they lacked any formal training in the science of music. It was a decided limitation in their musical education, though the debate goes on as to whether it harmed what might have been. It was not at all unusual for the pop music field to be ignorant of notes. Elvis did not read music, nor did a host of other talented singers of the era.

John seemed baffled whenever he got in a tight spot rehearsing in the studio. Surrounding him was an entire orchestra of people schooled in the art and science of music and he knew not the elementary notes on a keyboard.

*The Saturday Review* reported that George Martin, the Beatles' mix-master, technical adviser and producer, told of an incident one day while the group was recording with back-up instruments. John had requested a certain note from the saxophones. Martin instructed the saxophonists in what to play "and John interrupted."

"Look," said John, "I'm playing G but you're asking them to play B flat."

"That's right," Martin told him. "If they play their B flat, it sounds the same as your G."

"How's that?" asked a puzzled John Lennon. "Why doesn't it sound the same if they play G?"

"Well," said Martin, "it's because the instruments are in different keys and their B flat is the equivalent of your G."

"I don't know," said John, "sounds bloody silly to me."

Whether or not the Fab Four understood the science of music or not, they played well together and they were one of a very small group who wrote, played and marketed their own music.

One other aspect that became public knowledge was John's and Paul's concept of creative sounds. John mentioned to John Lukin, an actor in the first two Beatle films, about his experiences writing music with McCartney and that Lukin should write what he liked and hope the public would like it. Then John said that that was exactly what he and Paul had done, "and waited for the world to catch up."

The world never caught up. Following those first romantic sounds that met with rushed sales and the mobbing teenage crowd, there came into the Beatles a first-hand experience from popularity at a host of live performances.

The romantic love relationship was still there though now the music told us how much work it was to perform and create when "I've Been Working Like a Dog" hit. In the confines of the studio and as near prisoners in their apartments, both John and Paul began to reshape the music of the '60s to fit their scope. They had already, as Robert Hilburn wrote, "Started off by recycling the sounds of American rockers like Presley and Berry, but they showed amazing elasticity, stretching musically and thematically to add character and dimension to rock's simple foundations."

Lennon and McCartney had added spice and flippant words to their boasting sounds of "Help," and also to the desperate hopes of the generation when they wrote, "I Need Somebody." It was a shouting plea that went straight to the heart of the emotional generation of youth. John Lennon provoked the mind of the listener to a deeper awareness of the age. "I'm a Loser," or "You're Gonna Lose That Girl," and, of course, "I Have a Ticket to Ride." All of the flamboyance that spelled the Beatles could be summed up in two or three of their hits, but the team pressed on.

By 1967 with the creation of "Sgt. Pepper's Lonely Hearts Club Band" no serious student of the Béatles believed they were anything but creative and fresh. The composers' great skills were laid out before the eager listener in an array of new sounds that they infused into their music. Some of their cuts on their albums had back up sounds of guitars, ragtime piano, harpsichord, wrapping paper, scrub board, you name it. They used anything and everything in the studio to create the magic of new sound breakthrough. All of it they hoped would enhance their performance.

In the *Saturday Review*, Raymond Palmer commenting on the Beatles' recording sessions wrote: "The Beatles are always experimenting, trying to get new sounds, and this is why recording is their natural medium for expressing themselves. With the Beatles there is an experimental atmosphere in the recording studio because they use it as a musical workshop."

He was right. When they popped into the studio they had not arrived as artists rehearsed ready to record the product. They generally arrived early evening and experimented until the middle of the night on sophisticated sound equipment, with the studio and full staff working as if they were on recording time. If they dominated the studio, using crew and equipment lavishly hours on end, it was merely the way they saw the approach to great music. It was their type of work in workshop session. Besides, this method lent itself to a feeling of expectation.

At some of the studio sessions there was a childlike, thoroughly playful side of Lennon as reported in the *Sunday Mirror*. Fans seldom saw this side of John. Mickie Most, an actor in the Beatles' films, had taken his five-year-old son to the recording studio where the Beatles were pounding away on a rather boring session. John happened to notice the little boy and struck up a playful conversation. Suddenly John took a piece of white chalk and marked the lines on the studio floor for hopscotch." According to Mickie, his son played for an hour with John, "despite frantic calls for John to return to his studio, he and my lad played hopscotch together, without a care in the world."

The Beatles were not confined solely to the studio. There was a business to run as well.

John and Paul flew into New York City in May 1968 and proceeded to hold a press conference at the St. Regis Hotel. The writing seemed to be on the posh wall as they flicked ashes on the deep pile carpet and swigged beer. With feet up on the hardwood coffee table, Paul declared, according to *Newsweek*, that "We're in the happy position of not needing any more money."

"Yea," said Lennon, "everything we make now goes right to the tax man."

With that, they announced the formation of Apple Corporation Limited. They explained how "Apple" would include a recording studio, four feature films, stores and inventions in electronics. The only thing that would be excluded from the new corporation's direct sales would be distribution of records. They were still under contract to Capitol.

John let the newspeople know that the aim of the new business was not "a stack of gold teeth in the bank." A typical Lennon way of putting down the financial establishment. He went on to try to explain that their objective was to help new talent surface and to keep down costs. They served notice that the Beatles were not interested in becoming button-down managers. "This is business," said McCartney, "But we want to have fun doing it." In that spirit, they hired a Chinese junk and held their first U.S. board meeting while sailing around the Statue of Liberty.

Up to the point of "Yellow Submarine," the Beatles had moved from kinky sounds and blaring colors of words and music to the higher level of progressive rock. At this point with the introduction of "Rubber Soul" they fused experimentation with sounds that bridged classical to eastern. This was considered by many to be the greatest period of Beatle music. It all had a whimsical element of fun and games. At that point there dawned a new age of rock that others throughout the music industry would pattern and splash across the sound waves of the 70s until the pitch and fever abated after Mick Jagger and the Rolling Stones orgy of music in the '70s.

By the time such great hits as "Abby Road" and "Hey Jude" permeated the minds and ears of millions, people had begun to take the Beatles' and especially John Lennon's music seriously.

It was at that time that the Viet Nam war escalated and pacifism deeply ingrained itself in John's soul, and of course it surfaced in song—"All You Need Is Love." He laid out those words as his answer to the Johnsons and Nixons whom he felt were too establishment to care, but it gave the draft card burning youth and the protestors a rallying cry in music.

By the late sixties so many young people in the Los Angeles area had cheap ten dollar guitars that one young entrepeneur hitting the swap meets from Redondo Beach to Pomona sold Hong Kong imported guitars to make himself a millionnaire one year later. What were they singing with those cheap instruments across the world? "Yesterday," and "Strawberry Fields Forever."

John's total appearance kept pace with the times. Or perhaps it would be better to say he set the pace of the times by his very appearance. At first he wore the high buttoned suit and mixing bowl haircut. But that lasted but a brief period. John hated that look. He was even asked not to wear the glasses that he so desperately needed just to focus on scribbled sheets of words.

It had all been part of the Epstein image that John reluctantly accepted for a season and which caused him mental distress to think that he conformed. Early on, he even considered leaving the group so as not to be subjected to that common vote that dictated style of dress. There were times when John refused to go along with the group vote, especially after '67.

"We're not Beatles to each other, you know. It's a joke to us. If we're going out to the door of the hotel, we say, 'Right! Beatle John! Beatle George now! Come on, let's go!' We don't put on a false front or anything. But we just know that leaving the door, we turn into Beatles because everybody looking at us sees the Beatles. We're not the Beatles at all. We're just us." His point was that he wanted to look like himself as well. It was at that point that John put on his granny glasses and let his hair creep down to his collar and beyond.

Lennon's greatest weapon was humor, not appearance. He had a total lack of pretense and did nothing with the thought of trying to impress.

"I'm cynical about society, politics, newspapers... But I'm not a cynic," he insisted once to a UPI reporter, "As simple freaks of fame, however vast, the Beatles would have quickly expired. They remained because they were like no teenage idols before them: clear headed, sharp witted, above all endowed with the flash-quick repartee of their native Liverpool."

Discounting his own view of himself, John stood out as the quick witted sardonic Beatle. The renegade in John also made Liverpool dialect fashionable sounding. He spoke with his Liverpool lilt: "Y'see," "meself," "when somethin'," "trippin'," "It's disgustin', takin' me for a clean-cut lad." "y'know," "when I get fed op," "y'know," "Bein' a Beatle," "Thank veddy much," "Allo, wot? Wot? On wot? Oh, yeah, yeah," "y'know." The whimsey of John came partly from his native soil of the port city. He spoke with the barefaced silly little dialect that, until the Beatles came on strong, was thought to be lower class in London. Those from Liverpool, who wished to reach any heights of fame in London, first had to shed their dialect. Not Lennon. He spoke Liverpudian so totally that when the fame settled in, it became fashionable among the squired youth of London to mimic the Liverpool lilt.

John refused to be depersonalized. He was the working class hero and anyone that wished to join in with him had to accept him as he was. There were millions who wished to join him.

# 5

## John As Film Star

# 5

Some history becomes myth, some myth goes down in history, some statistics boggle the mind: the Beatles have sold, all over the world, upwards of 200 million records." There is no question that with those kinds of sales Beatlemania was big business. The records, however, did not represent the entire returns on their music. The Beatles' live performances were always sell outs, the published music by John and Paul, in tandem, made a staggering fortune and of course the endorsement of souvenirs and associated items of clothing, gear and toys all accumulated until some knowledgeable individuals estimated John's wealth in the 1970s at close to a quarter of a billion dollars. Money ceased to have any meaning at that point. If he wanted it, he got it whatever the price. Though John at times was personally embarrassed by his wealth, he still didn't just go out and give it away as some suggested. At one time in the heart of all the hit records, films and publishing, Lennon expressed concern to the Beatles about their looseness with finances. During the 60s he had no firm grip on just how much they or he alone was worth. It's interesting to hear Ringo Starr's perplexed comment to John's financial concerns while they were the Beatles:

"I don't know what John means when he complains about being short of money," Ringo said, a little bewildered when John tried to get an accounting. "We never need to carry any with us. If we want something we sign a piece of paper and ask them to send the bill to *Apple*. He has his car and his house and anything else he could possibly want."

It may have been that John wanted far more than money, whatever it was, he held onto the brass ring for yet more even though he thought seriously of leaving the group. The introduction of Allen Klien as business manager and Phil Spector as producer insulated the Fab Four from so much direct business involvement in their far flung corporate organization at that point, and the issue of finances seemed to take a secondary position of concern. The mother company was *Apple*. From its corporate offices all deals were initiated and ultimately consummated. By 1968, the Beatles' own financial organization handled everything. Nevertheless, there was a decided freewheeling attitude from John on down through the sizable organization, that money was limitless, though John never believed it. For one thing no one seemed able to determine the Beatles' total net worth of their self-created big business enterprise. This of course John wanted to know. He would have to be patient while he waited for that special person to come along who would be able to handle such affairs.

Whether an accurate accounting took place or not, John Lennon had the skills and the fame to make more money than he would ever spend and one of the methods of continued large earnings of Apple revenue was films.

Actually, John only participated in three films: "A Hard Day's Night," that tied in with the album of the same name; "Help," another music film; and his solo performance, "How I Won the War," a decided shift from the other two films.

The first two were roaring successes as was the music they were taken from. The third, not so. Keep in mind, however, that it was not a John Lennon film, rather a Beatles creation. Perhaps Richard Lester, an American film director, had as much to do with the raw, impish fun of the first two films as did the Beatles. He was a genius and the Beatles were wise enough to get him as their director.

Lester had been a child prodigy. He started school at 3 years old and wound up in college at 15. He was singled out for a television career after a romp through Europe that gave him experience and a more robust life, akin to the sort of life style John longed to have. At only 34, but completely in control, Lester launched the Beatles into their short-run movie career.

One of the key points to Richard Lester's friendship with John was Lester's commanding humor and completely natural ways. Lester frankly liked Lennon and John admired Lester as well.

Lester said of that experience of working with the Beatle films, "They allowed me to be what I damn well pleased. I didn't have to put on an act for them, and they didn't put one on for me."

After working with John on each of the films, Lester made this statement about the top Beatle, "I don't think he does anything with a conscious thought of trying to impress. He's remarkably free. He does not act the part."

In the first two films it was not so much John Lennon, movie star, as much as it was the Beatles as a group. "A Hard Day's Night" was a frolicking comedy. They must have had fun making the film because it came off as nothing more than that. It was the kind of harmless fun-film that went together in a hurry. They came up with the title song literally overnight.

The assistant producer said to John, "You know we really should have a song called 'A Hard Day's Night.'"

"Well, mate, where will we put it in the film?" John asked.

"Over the titles of the picture," the producer replied. "It'll help promote the picture and you'll have another song."

"When do you need it?" the perplexed John querried.

"We need it immediately."

It was about 10 o'clock at night when the request was made by the assistant producer. The next morning the same man was summoned to John and Paul's dressing room by the assistant director who mentioned that John wanted to see him. As he entered the dressing room there stood John and Paul with their guitars in hand.

"Hey man," John said excitedly, "We're ready, listen." John took a match book cover out of his pocket and put it on a table, then he and Paul proceeded to read the lyrics on the cover of the match book and sing, "It's Been A Hard Day's Night."

It became an overnight hit!

The "Yellow Submarine" was a Beatle film without Beatle participation, a totally different method of using their fame. It was amazing that it ever came off. But since it did not involve the Beatles in any film role, apparently it was acceptable to the organization. The "Yellow Submarine" was a feature-length cartoon with the sound of the Beatles, the dialogue track, dubbed by four Liverpudians who sounded a good deal like the Beatles. The director George Dunning proposed in a staff meeting that they ask the Beatles to write songs for the film, "to fill in a few specific places, but Good Lord! You just do not go suggesting words to John Lennon."

The "Yellow Submarine" was just one in a host of video releases that had the Beatle image front and center. They were on kiddie T.V. with 39 Beatles cartoons that went into several seasons at a profit. But for some strange reason, in 1967 during the holiday season, the Beatles' T.V. special, "Magical Mystery Tour" took a real thumping.

The decade was starting to close and with foresight, anyone, with an eye to the pop music scene of the '60s or the stuff that made up that whole throbbing era, could see that among the fatalities would be the Beatles. To dominate a decade was heady. Little more could be expected or even wanted. Still John persisted in giving more of self.

In the middle of all the hoop-la about the Beatles' music and films, there came on the scene John's first writing efforts. He titled his first published work, John Lennon, *In His Own Write*. John must have loved James Joyce, because the literary style was Joycian. Critics had little patience with John's effort; they put it down in a hurry as a style copy of Joyce. Of course, they reviewed the book because of its author. One critic mentioned that since the book would be read by "virtually the whole generation of adolescents in Britain and a good many in America, too," that maybe it was worth a glance.

Reviewing the second book that John scribed, *A Spaniard in the Works*, a critic mentioned very condescendingly that the adolescent of America and Britain would be able to read Joyce by proxy. Allowing for the fact that youths minds were usually only reached by "TV, radio, film, or the pages of a few popular newspapers," leaving a void in serious reading, the young non-reader would have a new insight into Joyce by way of John Lennon. The reviewers seldom took Lennon's literary skills seriously. They looked upon his book writing as pop art. John never published again as a literary figure after the second work. But no matter the critics, he did have fun with the English language, and it seemed to have been no small task to write an entire book in Joycian style.

In an interview about John's writing being Joyce-like, he denied any knowledge of the literary giant. Rather surprising from one who loved to play with words. If he had had no knowledge of Joyce he should have, for he would have loved *Finnegan's Wake*.

During the preparation of John's second book he had hired Victor Spinetti to help in the writing. It was a cold winter in 1968 that they worked in a freezing room in England. John suddenly turned to Victor with a question that was typically zany Lennon.

"Do you want to go somewhere warm?"

Victor thought he meant to another room where there might be an electric fire. "Instead, he picked up the phone and rang someone. A car arrived an hour later. At eleven that morning we were in Marrakesh in Morocco. We collected

Cynthia (Lennon's first wife) on the way to London Airport—but we took no money between us, only our passports. John only had to sign a bit of paper anywhere in the world and months later it would come back as a bill. So we didn't need money."

Then the topper came. For all their impetuous movements, said Spinetti, "When we got to Marrakesh we just fell about laughing because it was snowing."

So John was not only a rock and roll superstar, he was a hit film actor, and before the decade was over he became known in the press as the "Writing Beatle." That title would have fit whether or not the journalists meant books. John had already attained the title of composer.

"Lennon loved language," chimed in one tribute, "the sounds and rhymes and elastic elusiveness of words, and, like a dandy with a lace handkerchief, he liked to keep a pun up his sleeve." Even with that love of words, he one day turned to Dylan, who plead with John to listen to the words of Dylan's song. John responded with a rather unsettling reply, "I don't listen to the words."

It speaks well of John and Paul that in spite of the fact that they could not read a note of music nor had they ever taken any formal music lessons on their instruments, that they were totally uninhibited and to a high degree without form. Their ability to be the dream weavers had little to do with formal training. It was a sort of unbounded creativity that in the rushing sounds of the '60s had little structural form and discipline. Perhaps that accounts for their sudden acceptance by their fans who at first cared for merely a visual view of the Beatles.

Somehow, through all the hectic, wild days of films and music creativity, and a book or two tossed in, a pattern developed, coupled with a more disciplined method of madness. In short, the Beatles, more particularly John Lennon, captured the mood of the time. And frankly, it mattered little how skilled he was at the formal trade of composing or acting—everything he did sold. John, more so than the others, dwelt in a harried surrealistic world of sights and sounds.

When asked to define the style of music he produced during the Beatle era, John simply bowed away from the question. He had no answer. The critics claim his music was a complex jumble of every musical sound in the western world and even some eastern sounds: folk music, hymns, country, western, rock and roll, musicals, anthems, pop, opera, jazz; fun sounds, cynical music and lyrics, terror, love, hate, whimsical, and the list goes on to infinity. Why? Because he was unschooled in the art music and cared nothing about proper form.

The Beatles had more showmanship than any group of singers in years. Some believe more than in the history of the art. This contributed to their rapid rise in popularity. The predictions were that, yes, they would fade like a comet, but since they had such shine on stage, that expressed itself in spontaneity, fading would be slow coming. Said one observor, "...it has always remained their dazzlingly versatile music that has elevated them so far above the commonplace. Ever since the madness of the hysterical year 1963-64, their music has been with us, a perpetual lyrical accompaniment to the tempo of the sixties."

All in all it was John, more than Paul, who established the mood for the type of poetry contemporary youth would enjoy throughout the 70s and 80s, in part, because their brand of music expressed best the expanding images billowing from a life lived to the hilt and beyond.

# 6

## Experimenting With Meditation

# 6

Few people the world over have felt the pounding, pulsating, raucous life that John Lennon felt during the '60s. He had played all over Liverpool in grimy, sleazy dance halls with sweaty, unwashed bodies crammed into a hundred halls. His vibrant music offered him a way out. With a rise to international fame he saw crowds in the hundreds of thousands and still life was hectic. Nowhere could he go without someone reaching to grab, touch, push or fondle his body. The masses pressed in harder and harder. The excitement of the passion of nearly the entire world must have seemed surrealistic, and toward the end of the live appearances, unreal.

Is it any wonder that that young bewildered boy, later a man, sought escape? Like hundreds of actors and stars of the era, John experimented with mind altering drugs. First marijuana, then LSD and later cocaine. It's to his everlasting credit that by the time he graduated from the free-wheeling '60s he had conquered the imprisoning effects of drugs.

John once mentioned to the media that he had taken 1,000 LSD trips in the '60s. He told of music that had come out of those trips, such as "Cold Turkey." He admitted publicly that all the Beatles had been into drugs.

John, like the others, sought escape. The world had fallen at their feet and worshipped the Beatles. They had anything their minds and bodys desired. At this point in their stardom they frankly sought escape from the reality of the world that was so much with them.

This news, of course, upset the millions of fans whose lives had not yet been touched by the sweep of drugs. To those who had already experimented with everything the Beatles had tried, it merely confirmed their hunch that some of the music was an outcome of trips the Beatles had taken.

By August of 1967 the Beatles heard that the Maharishi Mhahesh Yogi was in London giving lectures on Transcendental Meditation. The Maharishi had come from his retreat in the mountains of India to spread his brand of belief to the British world. Some saw this as a relief from drugs. The lecture in London on peace and harmony opened up a new vista for the Beatles, and especially John and George. The stage was set for a totally new, drugless experimentation in mind altering meditation.

The whole group, Beatles, wives, and staff members responded to the lecture and were eager for deeper involvement in this new way of life. The Maharishi was flattered that the Beatles were struck by his belief. He invited them to attend his lecture series at the college in Bangor, North Wales. They made plans to spend the weekend in Bangor. When the word got out that the Beatles and their entire entourage were going by train to North Wales, the crush of fans and gawkers at London's Easton station, was worse than for departing royalty. Platform 8 was cordoned off with police officers to protect the Beatles. Easily half of the train's passenger cars were crammed with reporters and photographers on a lark to capture the Beatles latest infatuation with a religion.

At first the group, listening to meditators and teachers, found peace and joy in the instruction. The atmosphere at the school in Northern Wales lent itself to study. The only problem with the entire setting was the crush of media people outside clamoring to get shots of the Fab Four with the guru. Already news stories flashed across the globe telling of the mysterious Maharishi and his devoted following that now included the famed Beatles.

At noon the next day, after morning sessions in the art of meditation, the Beatles emerged. There came such a stir from the college courtyard which was filled with reporters that the Beatles were at last obliged to appear. The first thing they heard from one of the newsmen was his report that Brian Epstein was dead.

"Dead?"

Brian was like a father figure to the group. John had loved to frustrate the complex Brian. At times John actually had enjoyed watching the usually shy, poised Epstein squirm and stomp in a fit of temper. Though it was a known fact that John liked Brian very much and complimented him lavishly on his manager's business acumen.

Of late, Brian had had little to keep up his spirits. He had achieved the goal of establishing the Beatles firmly in the world's limelight as superstars. What else had there been for him to achieve? He had had boundless energy and loved throwing parties where he had invited famous people. That August day in 1967, when Brian had seen the group off for Northern Wales, he had still been youthful and talented. Yet, on his country estate he had accidentally taken a drug overdose and died alone.

The Maharishi learned of the death and invited the Beatles and friends into his private quarter at the college. The room was bedecked with tropical plants and fresh flowers. There he consoled them by explaining that Brian's soul was free to rise, that they should rejoice. In less than half an hour, in the presence of the guru, the entire group had regained their composure and were even laughing.

With great admiration for the Maharishi and a desire to find greater fulfillment in life, the Beatles and wives embarked on a pilgrimage to India the following late winter. They traveled en masse to the Maharishi's meditation training centre in mountainous Rishikesh. The new beliefs sunk deep into the absorbent mind of John as he practiced for hours the art of meditation. George, too, had a proclivity for Oriental thought, so he naturally found excitement in the sojourn in India.

They spent several weeks in the mountain retreat as students, living in an austere environment away from the clutter of the world. At first, it was bliss. They throve mightily on the mind soothing effects of the Maharishi and his faculty of trainers. For hours, the formerly bustling Beatles sat in meditation sessions that captured their thinking. Like so many new interests, John thrust himself into the meditation practice with total involvement and seemed to find great joy and peace to his soul. There were no drugs and no drinking, except for one smuggled bottle. John's thoughts even turned to resolving to be a better father and husband once he returned to England. It was in those serene environs that John wrote the lyrics and music to "Julia" in honor of his mother. Then the ugly rumor surfaced.

Someone passed the word that the Maharishi had an affair going with a lady. The word spread and most of the group believed it. John became angry over the hypocrisy of the guru. By the next day the Beatles and their entire group left the mountain retreat in a huff. John never forgave the Maharishi for his supposed acts of indiscretion. From that moment on, except for George Harrison, the Beatles never indulged in transcendental meditation again.

John and the others quickly thrust their pent up energies into the already created new business they had planned with Brian Epstein, known as Apple. It was the one they had announced on their trip to New York in 1968. They had declared to the world that Apple would become a kind of "Western Communism."

That concept seemed to alter as the unskilled musical team realized they had sunk millions of pounds into ventures that were simply not paying off. Without the skills of Brian to guard their financial interests and plead for caution, the Beatles made some unwise investments. Brian had foreseen in his planning for new ventures the year before, a chain of boutiques that would have swept across the western world. Perhaps Epstein, with his energy and business skill, could have made it pay. The Beatles did not.

The first of the planned boutiques was opened on fashionable Baker Street in London to the protests of shop owners along the street. The Beatles had turned loose four Dutch designers to conceive of and carry out the style and color of the new shop. So, in keeping with the flare of the hour, those four had the building painted with psychedelic colors. The protest from the media and the shop owners on Baker Street caused a downturn in business. The Beatles, lead by John, declared the shop a failure and gave away the 20,000 pounds in inventory, on the spot. It was a typical Beatle method of madness that befitted their reputation. Pandemonium ensued on Baker Street when the crowds descended to get a free gift.

The following year, Allen Klien became manager for the sprawling Apple business, even though Paul McCartney had opposed his appointment. Before the group was finished with their infighting, John let out the word that he was nearly broke and that the Beatles needed to get back to work.

The Beatles were hardly broke. They had mismanaged, and there were too many opportunists surrounding Savile Row where they had their studio, but their one record "Hey Jude" topped out at over six million worldwide record sales that year, and they had "Get Back" and "Don't Let Me Down," as solid hits; plus all the albums, films and music they had created for the past six years. All of this created sales running in the tens of millions. Plus, John and Paul held controlling interest in Northern Songs, their music publishing company.

If John needed cash, all he had to do was take up ATV's offer of nine million pounds for his and McCartney's share in the publishing firm. They rejected that offer and counter offered ATV 2.1 million pounds sterling for 20 per cent of ATV shares. They were trying to control Northern Songs.

All in all, the Beatles were well-heeled and doing great. For one thing, Brian had placed millions of pounds in trust funds for each member of the Fab Four. It was a nest egg that would come in handy when the eventual break-up would shatter their ties to one another.

# 7

## John and His Loves

# 7

The fact that John kept his marriage to his teenage love, Cynthia Powell, a secret for over a year indicates the type of relationship they shared. They got married in Liverpool in 1962. John, however, was a rising star in the record trade a few months after their quick wedding. It was the opinion of the Beatles and undoubtedly Epstein that the fans should not find out. It was the quiet, unassuming Cyn, as John called her, who stayed in Liverpool preparing to have their baby, while John was on the road.

Cynthia stood by, watching John rumble through those wild, maddening years of Beatlemania, peacefully caring for their new son, Julian. Oh, he moved her to a comfortable flat in London and even showed her off to the society of London. But he never seemed to mesh with her simple ways. She, in turn, seemed always a bit bewildered at her husband's rapid rise to international fame. She strolled through those years of intense public notice more as a spectator than one of the principals caught up in the aura of super-stardom.

Cynthia, through it all, remained the simple, clear-thinking clerk she had been at Woolworth's in Liverpool.

She was beautiful by anyone's standards. Her long blond hair and balanced facial features hankered back to the Marilyn Monroe look of the '50s. Perhaps of those surrounding the Beatle clan, Cynthia looked most like a movie star. Unfortunately, her's was a placid, rather easy-going manner that caused little if any excitement. It was Cynthia who got squeezed out by hordes of fans. She had trouble getting to her husband at times because she lacked the forceful personality to break through police lines. It was Cynthia who got left behind the cordoned off platform at the station in London when the Beatles left for Northern Wales. It was she who had to seek fans help to get past guards at the Beatles hotel in Miami. She had a beautiful spirit. It was she who was quick to forgive and usually came to the defense of the underdog. She tried to please John, though in her own statements she claimed that John expected too much of her. Her life revolved around watching others and sincerely admiring them for their talent. She was thrust into entertaining the superstars of the world as well as notable writers, speakers, and leaders of cults and she enjoyed watching those people with a sense of awe.

John, on the other hand, knew he was a cause, a force in the world that others would come to. Where Cynthia found contentment in peace, John ferreted out challenge and experimentation. She felt that John was "let down by her style of life."

It seemed inevitable that someone more suited for John's temperament and creative drive would wedge into the Lennons' life. It came in the form of a highly cultured, way-out lady from Japan.

There are those, and not a few, who insisted that Yoko Ono (in Japanese the name means ocean child) was the reason for the Beatle's break-up. If that was true, she was certainly one of the most influential women in the history of pop music. There was no question that Yoko Ono was the most powerful force in John Lennon's life. It was she who brought order into the grinding, often chaotic mess known as John Lennon.

Yoko Ono, born in Tokyo in 1933, came from a highly influential, wealthy family. Having risen to prominence through banking, her family had been traditionally Oriental until her parents, in particular her mother, who broke with tradition and became western in dress and manner. This Oriental-turned-Occidental from an ancient family of Japan set a role model for her daughter, Yoko, that allowed for experimentation in her young life. It was Yoko's mother who also broke with custom in the early 1930's and married for love. Yoko's father had longed to be a pianist, but wound up instead working in the family bank.

Yoko seemed always to be a timid figure. She remembered that her mother seldom was a mother. Because of her wealth and position, Yoko's mother could leave her oldest child along with her younger brother and sister in the care and keeping of servants. Yoko has said repeatedly to interviewers that she was not a happy child. Her mother was beautiful. She had taken on the appearance of a Hollywood film star, only very Oriental. Her face, like Yoko Ono's, was composed of the ancient Japanese features, passed down through generations of finely chiseled, classical beauties; except in her mother's case, set off by marcelled hair and short dresses.

All Yoko Ono wanted from her beautiful mother was love. She felt starved for love. Her mother, according to Yoko Ono, was like "having a film star in the house. When you're hungry and want food and someone says, 'Well, I'll show you a film of food,' you are never really fulfilled. It was like that, she was like somebody on a screen, always pleasant, always smiling at you, but she doesn't give."

Yoko remembered the pretense of having parents. Her father traveled a great deal while her mother danced and gave parties. She grew up a frightened child. The maids were angry with her and treated her in a mean manner. From Yoko Ono's vantage point in her parents home, she saw her mother in gaiety and her father in frustration. He was not what he had longed to be—a pianist. She watched her father spend hours at the piano.

Yoko attended an exclusive private school in Tokyo, along with her younger brother and sister. It had been the family's school for generations. Even the crown prince Akihito attended her classes. Shy, but bright, Yoko was first in her class even though she detested school and searched for ways to miss class, at times drinking hot tea to make herself ill. Through it all, she maintained a keen interest in poetry and writing, while her private governess taught her English, the Bible, music, Buddhist scripture, and a host of other related studies. Yoko tried to please her family, so she naturally did well in all subjects, convincing her family that she was a sound student.

Her education came to an abrupt halt when the fire bombing of Tokyo, at the peak of World War II, sent Yoko and her brother and sister into the countryside. The family thought it was best if the children remained in the farmlands for protection. Yoko was eleven and took charge of her brother and sister in spite of the fact that family maids had been assigned to watch after them. They struggled those desperate months, merely to stay alive. In the country they were reduced to begging from farm house to farm house for rice where the farmers viewed them as aristocrats, and many times refused to feed them. Yoko only remembers how hungry she was during that period of her survival.

After the war the family was reunited. Yoko's father had been able to retain the wealth of the family bank, despite the currency change that struck all Japan during the American occupation.

At nineteen, Yoko traveled to New York. Though she had been to America on holiday, at nineteen she decided to reside in New York along with her extended family. And, since her father was well known in banking circles and at the time of her arrival in New York, her uncle held the post of Japanese Ambassador to the United Nations, throughout New York's

Japanese society, Yoko was presented as "Mr. Ono's daughter" and the niece of the Ambassador.

It was always family. Yoko wanted to be known for her own talents as a poet or artist, anything to be herself and not merely a female object to be admired, especially the daughter or niece of someone important.

The problem with Yoko's poetry seemed to be centered in the very simple fact that she had never published any of her works. The same appeared to be the trouble with her art; she produced some things, but nothing she felt worthy to show. In New York, life took a new direction at twenty-four when she attended a "soiree musicale." At the showing she met a dazzling Japanese pianist, who appeared so gifted that she was caught up in a whirlwind courtship resulting in marriage to him.

The marriage was not to be enduring, and even though her new husband was famous, Yoko wanted her own career. When their relationship deteriorated, because of her husband's concerts and Yoko's desire for male companionship, she knew it was over.

She finally asked that her husband return to Japan, and there enjoy a great career. "I'm being such a bad strong wife to you," she confessed. He left and did make his life a success.

At that point in her existence Yoko schemed and devised a method for fame. She rented a loft at 112 Chambers Street in New York at $50.50 monthly—no lights or gas. There she created a "salon" to display her paintings. Since no one would accept her manuscripts, and record companies refused her singing talent, she decided to go on her own. Yoko completed a manuscript and printed up 500 copies of an art instruction book which she titled, "Grapefruit." In that interesting work were such innovative instructions as "Coughing Is a Form of Love." Her advice would assist the bored, especially those confined in prison. All one needed to do was make music, coughing. Or the ritual of "Painting to be Stepped On." A blank canvas that once was stepped on resulted in an invisible footprint on the mind. The art instruction in "Grapefruit" centered around one's mind or imagination. She showed people who visited the salon how to paint by lighting a match and burning canvases. Yoko called it "a smoke painting:" Strike match and place at edge of canvas then blow out fire and watch the smoke curl."

Or, the instructions graphically stated: "Instead of obtaining a mirror, /obtain a person. /Look into him...." The entire book consisted of personal acts that could be performed in a sort of puzzle of life. One entry in "Grapefruit" advised sending to friends a tiny piece of glass that had been shattered with a nail. Actually, the book, as well as the loft, became a showcase for her mind's landscape.

The loft became a showplace as well for what was heralded "The first loft concert." It was a snowy Christmas in the late 1950's that a number of prominent people showed up for the first performance. At that performance Yoko laid out her canvas and numerous people stepped on it, but no one noticed it as her canvas painting. Yoko was too shy to mention her painting.

One person did hear about Yoko's instructional paintings and invited her to a one-woman show at a Madison Avenue gallery. The smoke painting got a write up in the "Art News" as a new form of art.

In all her twenty-five years of painting, Yoko had sold a total of one painting for $25. Her music consisted of opera, mainly Japanese, and her poetry, live readings. There was no financial gain, yet by the early 1960's Yoko's name was established in the New York avant-garde circles with her paintings shown in some of the finest galleries. Plus, and it was an important plus, Carnegie Hall had performed her music.

When Yoko returned to Japan, to present her works there, she met with a bad review from a young American film maker that upset her confidence in her creative talents. The attack on her paintings, poetry and opera were so devastating for one so tender that Yoko attempted suicide and ended up in a mental hospital. One day, while recouperating, she met an American admirer who had traveled all the way to Tokyo to meet the artistic Yoko Ono. As a matter of fact, Yoko's former husband, Toshi, brought the man to the hospital. She was reluctant to meet the American, but Yoko's former husband talked her into it, thinking sincere admiration for one so talented as Yoko would help her state of mind.

She met, and in a short time married the film producer. As with the first marriage, so with the second, Yoko could not stand being too close with anyone, at least at that time in her life. However, she did get pregnant from her new husband. The baby was not wanted and Yoko sincerely felt that their offspring would merely cause her greater stress. She plead for an abortion. Her new husband, on the other hand, wanted the child. Yoko refused to love her new baby and when the child, a girl, was a year old Yoko left both baby and husband and returned to New York. The little family followed her a short time later, only to be rebuffed when Yoko showed little interest in them. She in turn left for London. They traveled after her. There was a scene in London causing Yoko's husband to take their daughter and leave for a vacation in the south of France. The three never lived together from that time on, even though they saw each other often.

It was 1966, the year Yoko's paintings hung in a gallery in London where the English loved her works. In fact, in London she was a celebrity, so naturally celebrities in turn came to see her and to view her creative efforts. Being a sensitive genius, quick to spot creative talent, John Lennon attended Yoko's showing. They met. John climbed a ladder to pound in a nail that was one of Yoko's contrived imaginary pieces of art. John told his hostess, after she informed him that he would have to pay to pound in the nail, and that he would use an imaginary hammer. They both felt an immediate response to one another. Yoko was seven years older than John, but the age difference made no impact to either as they fell in love. What did matter to Yoko was their disparity in fame. By the time they met, the Beatles were already known in the far reaches of the world, even the jungles of Borneo. (At Marudi, reached only by boat or air and airwaves, Beatlemania had settled into its Secondary School. There, students were waltzing, fox-trotting, and twisting to the only music they cared about: "I Want to Hold Your Hand," "A Hard Day's Night," "All My Loving," "Help.") With that sort of fame resting on John's shoulders it was not easy for Yoko to accept him. Her own fame was of a more narrow avant-gard circle as a result of her dabbling in the "highly unusual and unique." She wondered how they could possibly close the gap between their positions in world notariety. It appeared to be more academic than real. John was in love. Yoko possessed the spirit and challenge John had been searching for.

John kept a copy of "Grapefruit" on his bedstand, hoping to understand the fascinating Yoko with greater clarity. For some strange reason he never achieved the kind of peace through ritual that the book offered. He wondered, "Why is this woman telling me to do such mad things? ... I really thought that she was a fantastic, pushy, aggressive, Women's Liberation type of woman, from her work ... Then I found out she was a coward."

At first John moved cautiously in his involvement with Yoko. He determined that they would not be lovers or marry, rather they would work out a creative agreement through Apple Corporation to do a recording of Yoko as an artist.

She entered the studio and helped record. Her very presence in the studio caused bad vibes. The others, especially Paul, found her too disconcerting. As she accompanied John musically with her near operatic voice, the engineers, all except one who had worked opera, held their hands to their ears to shut out what they considered caterwauling.

The Beatles, nevertheless, persisted in their business arrangement. Almost everyone felt the intrusion of Yoko and found it jarring.

Yoko was never one to let things pass her by. She

constantly confronted her environment, no matter the cost. It seems reasonable to believe that Yoko and John blended together because of their total openness and disregard for decorum or diplomacy. Whichever way the public responded to Yoko she had the courage to go through with her own intense life.

# 8

## The Downfall

# 8

Some maintained that the "downfall" of the Beatles had started long ago, in part due to John's outbursts and silly lifestyle. True, there had been moments in the lives of the Beatles when John refused to play the role. It had always been Brian and Paul insisting on diplomacy and proper manners. Not John, he had grown tired of the whole charade. At times, John refused to hold back. The one time he should have and didn't brought down on top of him most of the fundamental Christians of the world. In an interview in 1966, prior to the Beatles' last concert tour, John outspokenly said, "Christianity will go. It will vanish and shrink. We're more popular than Jesus Christ..."

The tone of sarcasm and disrespect in that one statement sent thousands of Beatle records and albums up in flame. The cry and hue swept across the Bible belt of America like a fierce tornado, destroying, momentarily, all the adulation those Christian fans had heaped upon the Fab Four. The strange event turned against all four, not merely John. As John had surmised with his rise above Elvis in popularity, it was never solely John that caused the Beatlemania, it was his teammates as well. The group, like siamese twins, would have to suffer as well as Lennon.

The statement about Christianity and Christ were the kinds of off-the-cuff statements that John relished uttering. He enjoyed saying whatever popped into his head. He was little different than his mother in this respect. Up to that point the Beatles had been sell-outs wherever they toured and across the world they were the most popular group anywhere. It had been heady stuff. They had sung before royalty in London, been hosted by the internationally famous wherever, and had even been given the MBE award by the Queen of England. All in all, their public and private lives, thoughts and actions were flashed across the entire world overnight.

When John made his "more popular than Jesus" statement, even the interviewer who had pulled it out of him came to his defense. She stated what eventually became John's stock answer to the issue: "Lennon was simply observing that so weak was the state of Christianity that the Beatles were, to many, better known than Jesus."

The premise of the bumbling statement may have been accurate. They had sung to over 100,000 gathered in Manila. Their impact on the Orient and numerous youth throughout Asia Minor and Africa was astounding. In a very factual way, John may have been right. Christianity had not taken root in some of the countries where the Beatles were the hottest item in the music/entertainment market.

But John had learned first-hand that one simply does not blurt out such inflammatory statements without suffering aftershocks. Following his faux pax, he had felt the seriousness of his statement each day when he arose at 2 o'clock in the afternoon. Cynthia would have sorted through the day's mail by that time and John, in a kind of stupor, would ask, peeking over her shoulder, how the mail was going—pro or con? The fact that so many people were up in arms with what he had said bothered John greatly. It also upset Brian Epstein, who had constantly feared a sudden decline of the Beatles popularity.

Brian had tabulated the response from America, where the statement had its greatest fall out, and decided he had best do something quick. If the trend to burn records in the streets, or spread the ban on Beatles' music on the radio, which had started with Station WTUF in Birmingham, Alabama then had spread to at least six other states; then who could say that one statement could very well cause the downfall of the Beatles. Brian flew to New York where he made apologies for Lennon's statement by indicating that John had not meant that the Beatles were greater than Jesus. He meant that at that moment perhaps they were better known than Jesus throughout the whole world.

Even John saw the wisdom in clarifying his bombshell statement. When he arrived in America to begin the Beatles tour in 1966, he made it clear in a press conference that he regretted that so many had misunderstood the meaning of his comment.

Like so many of John's outbursts, that, too, passed. However, it had caused scars to remain on the Beatles team effort so that by 1970 the gap had widened between all four Beatles.

It had been John who stood out as most eccentric among the four. One interviewer noted that, "John Lennon was the one whose mind was constantly running like a generator keeping some essential service going. He was the one who would loll back in a chair, his knees drawn up nearly level with his ears, and pick out tunes on a mandolin while he was talking to you—not out of rudeness (though he could be as rude and hurtful as a caveman's club) but because he simply liked functioning on two levels at once."

Already John had espoused other causes that he must have known were incompatable with the other three. But not merely the Beatles were effected by his changed life. He left his wife Cynthia for Yoko Ono. He had experienced instant fame, acid, meditation, so at that point, he and his new wife

Yoko were caught up in the Peace Movement.

The Beatles, in their private lives, had actually drifted into separate ways by 1969. They were still coming back together to make their hits, though each felt free to record, entertain or simply relax as he chose. With John, it was the Peace Movement.

In March 1969, John and Yoko got married at Gibraltar. They had taken a day trip from Paris to the British commonwealth shore of the rock. Immediately, they determined to make of their honeymoon a statement of peace by throwing open their hotel bedroom to reporters. In a move to demonstrate for peace, they stayed in bed for seven days at the Amsterdam Hilton where they answered reams of questions. The "Bed-in," as it was dubbed, became a symbol of their efforts for peace. The whole affair that was more comedy and laughter than serious demonstration was viewed with chuckles by most of the reading/viewing public. It nevertheless set the tone for John's and Yoko's peace drive and gave it the pop fame some hoped would happen. The pair tried hard to impress the world with this new found conviction. On April 1, 1969, John and Yoko showed up at a press conference in Viena following the premiere of an Apple film, "Rape," wearing white pillow cases. It was still part of the "Bed-in." There, as they had done in Amsterdam, they spoke of love and peace, while eager media people broadcast it to the entire globe.

John was into his new era of folk "revolution." He, and now Yoko, were seen everywhere thumping for peace. The Viet Nam War was ready made for John's type of crusade.

John and Yoko appeared that year in Montreal, Canada where they recorded peace music, held press conferences and radio interviews. The reason for Montreal was simple. Because of a marijuana conviction in London the year before, John was not eligible for a visa to enter the United States. While parked on the border in Canada, though, John reapplied for permission to enter the U.S. He truly wanted to re-enter the country. Lennon loved the United States.

Besides, in the U.S. he would have greater impact by demonstrating for peace.

The U.S. refused to budge on the issue. Many in America felt it was Nixon who put the tight lid on John not getting in. Before the group packed up to return to London, John, optimistic to the end, said, "I'm sure we'll get there ... It's just a matter of under what conditions. We won't play games with the guv'ments."

John hit out at violence, and like a Martin Luther King, he abhorred it. From Canada he pleaded with the youth of America to avoid violence to achieve their ends. He said in one news conference, "The only thing they can't control is the mind, and we have to fight for sanity and peace on that level. But the students have gotten conned into thinking you can change it with violence and they can't, you know, they can only make it uglier and worse."

With a refusal even from Canadian authorities, who asked them to leave, the Lennons returned to their recently purchased 72-acre estate called Tittenhurst Park at Ascot. For all their peace and freedom they were well-heeled and able to live like the wealthy establishment types they so opposed.

Musically in the latter '60s, John had done some work with the Beatles, but his heart was tied up in the music he and Yoko could make together. Prior to the Canadian peace trip, he had released the first non-Beatle album called "Two Virgins" LP. It was legal for him to do so provided he released the album under the Apple label. The album was controversial to say the least. The cover, if nothing else, caused a stir. There in stark black and white stood John and Yoko, naked. It was anything but sensual, with bodies beginning to show the thickness of growing middle age. The photo seemed to be an attempt to strip away every vestige of privacy and let the whole world see that they would hide nothing. Actually, the whole scheme seemed to hark back to the avant-garde, with Yoko trying for something shocking and original. All in all, it was the era of "let it all hang out," and so they did.

Paul McCartney was outraged with Lennon's brand of behavior. He had always been more proper than John about such matters of taste, even though he, too, dabbled in drugs. The music of "Two Virgins" was weird and to Paul, the cover obscene.

Their next musical release in 1969, "Unfinished Music No. 2—Life with the Lions," gave the listener, who ventured to buy it and listen, yodeling by Yoko and screeching feedback guitar by John. Also, the album included a singing of the newspaper by Yoko and hospital sounds of Yoko's miscarriage.

By summer, "The Ballad of John and Yoko" was released as a Beatles record and it made the charts. Later that season, John released the rally song of the Peace Movement, "Give Peace a Chance." This enduring anthem was written and recorded for the protestors and common people everywhere. John said of it to a *Ramparts* reporter, "I felt an obligation...to write a song that people would sing in the pub or on a demonstration."

His flirting with left-wing politics and a search for release from what he described as "humiliation" being a Beatle, lead directly to the astounding hit, "Come Together." It was music for the Utopian dreamers. The kind of tune a communal group could hum in the cornfield.

There were other releases by John and Yoko, with the background being what they titled, "The Plastic Ono Band." The music tended to be a collage of all their experiences up to that time. One of the outstanding releases that endured the decade of the 70s was titled "Cold Turkey." It expressed John's wailing of drugs through his Beatle fame years.

Most of the music of that year and, for that matter for the next three years, was summed up by the chroniclers as self-confession in song. It also helped to signal the downfall of the Beatles.

# 9

## Fight His Youth

# 9

One evening John Lennon got a quick call from Paul McCartney. Paul said in the course of their brief conversation, "I've decided to leave." As *Life Magazine* said later, "The pop world's greatest partnership was thereby dissolved."

It was the timing of the event that bothered John the most. He had made up his mind as early as '66 to leave the Beatles, though for reasons only John knew he had stayed on the merry-go-round with his three brethren. Now all of a sudden it was Paul who pulled the plug. What timing! John's only comment to the press, at first, was to credit Paul with a great sense of p.r. and headline grabbing.

The Beatles experienced a gradual break-up. To the public it may have appeared to be sudden. To John, however, it had been on the way since 1966. When Pete Seeger, the folk singer, wailed away with "Give Peace a Chance" to the quarter of a million gathered at the Washington Monument, it was clear to those alert enough to read the writing that John had Yoko, and they together had no need for the Beatles.

For some reason, many did not anticipate the break-up. Some insisted that without the group the individuals would shrivel up and blow away. *Time* quoted Lester's description of the Beatles as "'the four-way multiple plug-in personality,' in which each one is only a phase of a larger unit that has far more reality for them than any other human relationship they know."

Because in the minds of most fans and interpreters, the Beatles were one. And their style of music and pop artistry eminated from the group. Which was to say that any break-up, especially between John and Paul, would destroy any future musical innovations. Without the synergism of the whole, the parts would dissolve into mere ordinary music. That was what they thought, but John, especially, proved the critics wrong. It took a seasoning period, and he nearly destroyed himself in the process, but John, as well as Paul, proved to be versatile enough alone to show creative talent.

John had a phrase for the break-up: "The dream is over." He labelled it "a myth." To many, the Beatles had been far more than a myth. To an entire generation of youth, they represented the cultural core of their very real teenage lives. The Beatles were the substance of many dreams, so naturally the break-up hit headlines across the world and caused a collective uproar and sense of disunity in an already strained world of conflict and separation.

Actually, Beatlemania ended with the final tour the Beatles made to America in the mid-sixties. Though the music persisted and fans never abated, the storming crowds had already passed into pop history. The screaming girls of the Beatlemania era had grown to maturity with the more mature sounds of the Beatles.

When Apple's press officer, Derek Taylor, announced that Paul McCartney had broken with the Beatles because of "personal, business, and musical differences," that statement merely added fuel to the hot debates among the fans that Yoko was to blame. There were death threats sent to Yoko Ono. She naturally became the object of much distrust and outrage. People were calling her the "dragon lady." Some maintained that she had a mystic mental grip on John that he was helpless to resist. Yoko's solemn manner and sly smile did nothing to allay that mood of distrust and resentment.

There was the residue of music sung by the Beatles yet to be released through the remainder of the year and on into the next. Three weeks after Paul's declaration of leaving, the top hit "Let It Be" and later "The Long and Winding Road" were immediately in demand. One survey reported that the third release, "For You Blue" sold 1.2 million copies in two days in the U.S.

One other person surfaced in the news as a cause of the split—Allen Kline. According to *Newsweek*, "The breakup had been a long time developing. One cause was the importation a year ago of an American, Allen Kline, who made all kinds of promises to clear up the muddle of the Beatles' financial affairs. McCartney not only could not abide Kline personally but thought that Kline had botched the Beatles' business. Derek Taylor also mentioned, "It was easier for four boys to get together than four men and four wives."

Whatever the real cause of the split, Allan Kline let Paul know that as far as the business end was concerned, the Beatles were under contract until 1976.

There followed a series of "friendly" law suits by McCartney to get what was his and also to have his own independent company. He had already released his best selling, "McCartney" LP that itself sold over one million copies in a month. John and Paul together sued Northern Songs for half of the company's total receipts. The court problems persisted for years.

The whole tenor of the Apple organization of the early 1970s was split. It seemed that each of the Beatles was happy to make the break. John had told a reporter much later that each one of the four had threatened to leave before Paul made his statement public. No one can read into any statement Lennon made that he was sorry to see the breakup. Once it happened, he was the greatest opponent of reunion. "It's over," he kept repeating whenever someone would ask if there was any impending Beatles comeback.

Not only the Beatles were shattered as myths of the '60s. John broke with the Peace Movement as well in the early '70s. Lennon had become increasingly irrate with the treatment Yoko had received from a host of sources. Not only the media and fans accused her of interfering in John's life, word leaked out that the former Beatles felt the same way. Lennon didn't take lightly to the way people put down Yoko.

It was as if he planned to take his fragile bride to New York where they both hoped to find hope and turn their backs on most of their former interests. John saw the entire former decade as a myth—"the generation thing." He was fed up with meditation, drug trips, peace and the "whole bag and baggage" of the era. In protest he shaved off his beard and trimmed his hair. "I'm sick of all these aggressive hippies or whatever they are... They're under the delusion of awareness by having long hair, and that's what I'm sick of."

John put down the intellectuals, the vast middle class and even his fans. *National Review* mentioned that John claimed, "The music—the good music they made together—stopped when they stopped doing all night club dates and began, having become famous, to do concerts for vast audiences."

The revolution of the '60s was over before the Beatles' break-up. Like so many things John tied into, he was never the leader or the spearhead, except with the Beatles. He played the role of cheerleader. The drugs, the rock and the innovations that came were already there, he merely interpreted them and pumped hot air and sound into the mood. His strengths were in words and sounds. Perhaps one of the attractions above all else that he felt for Yoko Ono was her spirit of avant-garde. She had the ability to lead. Hers was truly a life of break-through and experimentation. It was no wonder that he was captured by her total life-style.

In the early '70s, John brought Yoko to New York where they could lose themselves in the one city they felt understood them. U.S. Immigration had granted John a temporary visa, yet he would have problems with that issue for five more years. The Lennons made a direct path to an outstanding doctor whom they sensed had the cure they sought to heal their lives. They fell under the spell of John (The Primal Scream) Janov who took the two into deep therapy where he forced the Lennons to feel accumulated pain erupting from their childhood. Lennon said of that therapy, "I had to do it to really kill off all the religious myths." According to John the process was excruciatingly painful.

Janov convinced the Lennons that their fears had been instilled in them by their environment and early childhood. John sat for days reading and repeating all the hundreds of songs he had ever written. The realization of what he had written nearly overwhelmed him with the amount of energy he had poured into that one area of his life. Most of what Janov pulled out of John was labeled "ugly." When the final sessions creeped up, John also saw that he had not been wanted as a child which he equated with lack of love.

In a recapping of that therapy, John explained to Blackburn and Ali, two interviewers for *Ramparts*, "This lack of love went into my eyes and into my mind. Janov doesn't just talk to you about this but makes you feel it—once you've allowed yourself to feel again, you do most of the work yourself. When you wake up and your heart is going like clappers or your back feels strained, or you develop some other hang-up, you should let your mind go to the pain and the pain itself will regurgitate the memory which originally caused you to supress it in your body. In this way the pain goes to the right channel instead of being repressed again, as it is if you take a pill or a bath, saying, 'Well, I'll get over it.'"

After therapy the Lennons settled back in New York. From that experience came love for a season. John wrote and sang what amounted to one of his greatest poetic works, "Imagine."

Also, among some of the more sentimental gush that came from those sessions was his release of "My Mummy's Dead,"

"Remember," and "Love." He still clung to the aftertaste of shattered youth.

# 10

## Settling In

# 10

Never had Lennon supposed that he and Yoko would break up. Then suddenly the world learned that, in 1973, she wanted him out! Perhaps no one will ever piece together all of the happenings in the Lennon camp that sent John packing to a lost year and a half away from Yoko. The events leading up to the booting are not clear. All Yoko or John would say about the causes leading up to the separation were elusive statements about his actions that troubled her greatly.

Yoko had grudgingly accepted her role as mother figure and tutor of John. John acquired a dependency on Yoko that few men of his status in life had ever allowed to happen. It's clear that Yoko had deep insights into the unusual thinking of John and frankly the ability to correct the flaws that caused him such pain.

John saw himself as a working class person, and Yoko accepted that. He had the capacity to lose himself in day to day pursuit of ordinary happening, but those traits were not being allowed to surface.

Yoko Ono Lennon with her maternal love to give

apparently felt frustrated that John, who needed the nourishment of that type of love, was simply not yet ready to receive it. It undoubtedly was this aspect of their lives that caused the separation.

John left, thinking he was free of her, and that he would have the freedom to shatter his life in any way he wished. Perhaps there was a feeling of losing his youth and a desire to recapture some earlier fantasy. Whatever his thoughts he did leave with a feeling of glee, like a boy out of school.

Yoko, for her part, was willing to wait. She had done without him before they were married, she called herself a "moving on person." She would do just fine in his absence.

It took only a few months for John to realize that being out of school was not truly freedom. John referred to that period of months as his "lost weekend." In the two interviews he granted in the fall of 1980 with *Newsweek* and *Playboy,* John Lennon eluded to those eighteen months that he and Yoko were separated. "She kicked me out." It was like being stranded "in the desert" or "adrift at sea." He spoke, also, of how he left for California where he invited into his house lively and raucous friends: Harry Nilsson, Keith Moon and a host of in-and-out people. Fun seekers all, they sank to near loonies in a madhouse of booze and parties. John lost all sense of responsibility to anyone, yet he kept in touch with Yoko by phone. He would plead with her to let him return home, realizing he was trudging through a desert of puffy ashes. "No" was the constant answer. "You're not ready."

*The New York Times Magazine* wrote a small piece in summary of where—and—how are they now? It casually reported that John Lennon "is living in New York apart from his second wife, Yoko Ono, and is fighting a three-year-old battle against the Government's attempt to deport him because of a British drug conviction. He has had a hit single ("Whatever Gets You Through the Night") and a hit album ("Walls and Bridges")."

Somewhere in the course of John's madcap test, Yoko had sent John on a trip around the world either before the year and a half's separation or very close to the end. At least, he did find himself in the Orient. According to John's accounts, given two separate interviewers, he told of being isolated in his hotel room in Hong Kong where he claims to have taken forty baths to ease his emotions. While bathing one morning, he glanced out at the city of Hong Kong, a moving sensation of personal awareness swept over his body, then a revelation came to him, "It's me." he said. To Lennon the sensitive individual, it was like discovering God. He shouted to himself, "It's me!" He quickly called Yoko and repeated into the phone. "Guess who, its ME! It's ME here."

He had a sensation of liberation envelop his whole being and, according to his account, he walked out into the streets and onto a commuting ferry among strangers who did not recognize him as John Lennon. That experience of non-recognition by those about him also gave him a sense of freedom. For so long he had been "John Lennon, the famous Beatle." He saw for the first time in a decade that it was possible to move freely among ordinary working class people. He spent several days shopping in Hong Kong without anyone realizing he was John Lennon. "...it was fantastic."

The experience of soul searching led John back to Yoko in late 1974. It was an evening at the Elton John concert that John saw his wife backstage. Lennon had teamed with Elton John on Elton's cutting of "Lucy in the Sky with Diamonds." The two appeared on stage at Madison Square Garden singing "Whatever Gets You Through the Night," "I Saw Her Standing There," and "Lucy in the Sky with Diamonds."

When John and Yoko met in the semi-public glare of dozens of people, the same feelings of respect for one another that they had experienced in their years of marriage sent them into each other's arms.

The media mentioned that in March of '75 John and Yoko were back together. It must have been a joyful reunion, from it came their only child whom they named Sean Ono. After three miscarriages this was a great blessing to their reunited lives.

In a matter of months things were looking up for John's

alien status in the United States. John had gone to court in the summer of '74 to explain that the ousted Nixon administration had made a special point of trying to deport him because of his old antiwar stance during the Peace and Freedom era that they wrapped up a package of a drug arrest. His legal advice found a technicality in the law that spelled out "marijuana arrest" and not cannabis resin that he had been arrested for in London in '68. The Lennons, especially John (Yoko had not been convicted on the same charge in England) had tried every way they could to maintain a foothold in the country on a visitor status to avoid deportation. One of the main reasons Yoko plead for their stay was to look for her daughter, Kyoko Cox. Yoko had maternal desires to see her daughter who was with her father hiding out somewhere in the United States. When Yoko and Cox had been divorced, the court had not awarded sole custody to either parent. Once Cox had wrenched his child from Yoko, at an earlier court scene in Spain, he had taken the child into hiding.

Yoko persisted in pleading with immigration to allow John and her to search for her child. After all, by 1974, Yoko had been able to reverse the Spanish court decision and receive permanent custody of Kyoko. The trick was to find the child.

The search for the daughter went on while John fought his case to remain in the country. He had the finest paid legal staff that he could find. So with that type of power, in time, they got the government to take a serious look at the old marijuana conviction and drop all efforts to deport him. John was granted a green card in the summer of 1976, thus giving him "permanent resident alien status."

Except for the lack of finding Kyoko, the Lennons settled happily into their new home off Central Park West, The Dakota apartment building. Up to that time they had been housed in Greenwich Village, in a two-room apartment. They sought and found the kind of apartment building they both loved. It was an old nineteenth-century brownstone building that had a certain class that was so essential to

## Settling In

Lennon's life style. It was called The Dakota due to the distance people traveled in the 1880s to get out to Central Park West from the old downtown.

The Dakota apartment building, when it was completed in 1884, was tauted as "the most beautiful apartment house in the world." The building carried a legacy of accidents and strange happenings, however. Eccentrics had lived in some of its rooms long before the Lennons moved into the massive seventh floor apartment No. 72. At one time, a former tenant was alleged to have buried $100,000 in bills in the concrete, four-foot-thick floor beneath the Lennons new living room.

When the Lennons came to buy their apartment, the gabled roofline of the Dakota was a preferred building for show biz and comfortably wealthy people: Judy Holliday, Lenard Bernstein, Robert Ryan, the former star, Judy Garland, and others had once lived there or were still residents when the Lennons settled in. Of late, the glamorous, though massive old building had been the backdrop for the filming of "Rosemary's Baby."

The Lennons met with some resistance when the tenants learned the former Beatles star had bought No. 72. Naturally the low profile tenants felt that the Lennons would throw wild parties, upsetting the decorum of the residence and they were merely guarding their privacy. They were wrong, of course. The Lennons had bought hoping to find a similar life in the heart of New York. They, too, sought a life free from any such behavior. The only unusual Lennon happening was a seance they held to communicate with spirits of the former residents. Yoko claimed to have contacted Jessie Ryan a former owner who had died some years earlier. Yoko reported to the Ryan family the whereabouts of Jessie. They were not impressed.

The Lennons had their massive apartment renovated to suit their needs. John wished to embark on a new venture in life, so he constructed the most complete, up-to-the-minute kitchen the apartment complex had ever known. He had called in a designer, Paul Segal, who installed every conceivable appliance and gadget known to the culinary arts. The kitchen itself had white walls and baked brick floor. A long wooden table with white directors chairs made it comfortable.

Over the following years, John and Yoko bought up every available apartment in the building that came up for sale. Some feared that the Lennons planned to buy up the entire block-long building. Who knows, perhaps they did. In their apartment or in additional rooms they had purchased they housed their outstanding collection of Egyptian art objects along with sound equipment. Some maintained that the apartment had the appearance of a museum.

Yoko, of course, had her plans as well. She took up a suite of offices on the ground floor so she could carry out her new task of making the Lennons' businesses pay. She enjoyed the feeling of nature and had her office ceiling painted to appear as if it were the sky.

The Lennons stayed close to home for the next five years, except for a trip to Japan to show their new son to his grandparents and a trip to Europe. For the next five years they devoted their considerable talents to making The Dakota truly a home and Yoko's office the center of their large business. Each decided to swap roles during that "settling down" time. John opted to retreat to the running of a household. He became what is later decribed as a "househusband." Yoko took up the task of running the family business.

She, an avid chess player, saw business as an extension of her favorite game. Yoko was inherently capable of handling all the financial affairs of the enterprises. With her family background in banking, it's doubtful she ever felt incapable of transacting complex business arrangements to protect John's millions. John had never claimed to have any skill at caring for his wealth. He surely experienced relief from spending a decade trying to consolidate his holdings. Now miraculously, he did not have to worry about the financial interests of

Apple. His was an absolute trust in Yoko's abilities to handle it.

At first Yoko had to make it clear to the business managers and legal representatives that she and not John was key director on the board. They learned quickly that she could dismiss people in rapid-fire order with the iron will of a king, though she preferred to cooperate with the high paid financial guardians if they would see reason. She worked diligently tallying up the Lennons' far-flung interests with daily trips downstairs to her expanding office facility. Much like a banker or broker on Wall Street she applied herself to the work at hand.

Yoko gradually shifted the Lennon interests from investments in publishing and recordings to real estate and dairy cattle. Before she made public some of the deals, news reports mentioned that the Lennons had acquired dairy cattle and holdings valued at 60 million. One evening John read in the newspaper where Yoko had sold a cow for a quarter of a million dollars. That deal nearly popped the buttons off John's shirt with pride in his shrewd wife's transactions.

From the moment Yoko took over active control of the Lennons' holdings, John seemed to concern himself no more with that area of his life. What he did achieve and achieve to perfection was feed and tend to little Sean, as well as cook the meals. He relished the idea of learning the true role of a traditional mother and wife, and that in the course of his day, meant baking bread and changing diapers. Of course, he was assisted by a staff of servants that would have pleased any housewife, still in all, the fact that he participated, took responsibility and directed offered him a sense of comaraderie with the souls of countless housewives throughout the world.

Life took on simple pleasures for the Lennons. John loved television and likely spent many hours watching shows, especially the Johnny Carson show. He mentioned once how impressed he was that the entire world could be brought to his feet by the click of a button.

This was a time of reflection and reconstruction for both John and Yoko. He constantly fought myths about himself. In The Dakota he may have found a way to fight hero worship. He knew that there was a necessity for demystification. When work abated he would sit in bed and look out at the sky and dream. Surely he pondered his past.

"I really thought that love would save us all," he said, speaking to an interviewer for *Commonwealth*. In that same interview, Lennon stated, "My life is dedicated to living, just surviving is what it's about, really, from day to day.... Just surviving is the rock-bottom password of this prolonged moment.... And so good friends, you'll just have to carry on."

John, more than any of the top singing stars, was into love. He believed in love. Said the *New Yorker* of John's brand of love, "For John love is no lofty agape; it's longing, deprivation, protectiveness, and has-this-really-happened-to-me awe." Those were the things of his dreams.

John never stopped viewing himself as "a basic working class person." He expressed a number of times that if he were a hero then he clearly was a "working class hero," a child of the working class. He often referred to that missing element of love in his life. He maintained that as a child, "I was never really wanted." *Ramparts Magazine* got him to reveal some of his deepest feelings about his loneliness when he declared, speaking of why he was able to achieve superstardom, "The only reason I went for that goal is that I wanted to say: 'Now, mummy, daddy, will you love me.'"

John and Yoko both held a strong belief in an after life. Granted it was a tailored belief that he fashioned to fit his mode of madness, but the belief was firmly entrenched in his whole being. He sensed deep within himself that life continued beyond mortality. That he would absolutely be a force in life beyond this life.

It's ironic that The Dakota apartment building was the Lennon's haven of love and tranquility, where he truly came to grips with his own reality. Once he had declared that, "I'm not sure where my place is." It seemed to many that he found that peaceful place where he and Yoko created it at The Dakota. Their life at The Dakota since they dropped out of public glare to find themselves as a family became, for worldwide fans, a silent movie without captions.

In 1979, with fans still begging to know how the Lennons were doing hidden away in their apartment building, John and Yoko took out an ad in the *Times* that detailed some of their private activities and more especially their feelings. They titled it "A Love Letter From John and Yoko to People Who Ask Us What, When, and Why."

"The past ten years we noticed everything we wished came true in its own time, good or bad, one way or the other. We kept telling each other that one of these days we would have to get organized and wish for only good things. Then our baby arrived! We were overjoyed and at the same time felt very responsible. Now our wishes would also affect *him*. We felt it was time for us to stop discussing and do something about our wishing process: The Spring Cleaning of our minds! It was a lot of work. We kept finding things in those old closets in our minds that we hadn't realized were still there, things we wished we hadn't found. As we did our cleaning, we also started to notice many wrong things in our house: there was a shelf which should have never been there in the first place, a painting we grew to dislike, and there were the two dingy rooms, which became light and breezy when we broke the walls between them. We started to love the plants, which one of us originally thought were robbing the air from us! We began to enjoy the drum beat of the city which used to annoy us. We made a lot of mistakes and still do. In the past we spent a lot of energy in trying to get something we thought we wanted, wondered why we didn't get it, only to find out that one or both of us didn't really want it. One day, we received a sudden rain of chocolates from people around the world. 'Hey, what's this! We're not eating sugar stuff, are we?' 'Who's wishing it?' We both laughed. We discovered that when two of us wished in unison, it happened faster. As the Good Book says—Where two are gathered together—It's true. Two is plenty. A Newclear Seed.

"More and more we are starting to wish and pray. The things we have tried to achieve in the past by flashing a V sign, we try now through wishing. We are not doing this because it is simpler. Wishing is more effective than waving flags. It works. It's like magic. Magic is simple. Magic is real. The secret of it is to know that it is simple, and not kill it with an elaborate ritual which is a sign of insecurity. When somebody is angry with us, we draw a halo around his or her head in our minds. Does the person stop being angry then? Well, we don't know! We know, though, that when we draw a halo around a person, suddenly the person starts to look like an angel to us. This helps us to feel warm toward the person, reminds us that everyone has goodness inside, and that all people who come to us are angels in disguise, carrying messages and gifts to use from the Universe. Magic is logical. Try it sometime.

"We still have a long way to go. It seems the more we get into cleaning, the faster the wishing and receiving process gets. The house is getting very comfortable now. Sean is beautiful. The plants are growing. The cats are purring. The town is shining, sun, rain, or snow. We live in a beautiful universe. We are thankful every day for the plentifulness of our life. This is not a euphemism. We understand that we, the city, the country, the earth are facing very hard times, and there is panic in the air. Still the sun is shining and we are here together, and there is love between us, our city, the country, the earth. If two people like us can do what we are doing with our lives, any miracle is possible! It's true we can do with a few big miracles right now. The thing is to recognize them when they come to you and be thankful. First they come in a small way, in everyday life, then they come in rivers, and in oceans. It's goin' to be all right! The future of the earth is up to all of us.

"Many people are sending us vibes every day in letters, telegrams, taps on the gate, or just flowers and nice thoughts. We thank them all and appreciate them for respecting our quiet space, which we need. Thank you for all the love you send us. We feel it every day. We love you, too. We know you are concerned about us. That is nice. That's why you want to know what we are doing. That's why everybody is asking us What, When, and Why. We understand. Well, this is what we've been doing. We hope that you have the same quiet space in your mind to make your own wishes come true.

"If you think of us next time, remember, our silence is a silence of love and not of indifference. Remember, we are writing in the sky instead of on paper—that's our song. Lift your eyes and look up in the sky. There's our message. Lift your eyes again and look around you, and you will see that you are walking in the sky, which extends to the ground. We are all part of the sky, more so than of the ground. Remember, we love you.

John and Yoko Ono<br>May 27, 1979 New York City"

In the summer of 1980 John and a crew of five sailed a yacht from Newport to Bermuda. It was a harrowing trip. At one point in a storm John took control of the helm. At length they arrived safely in Bermuda. It was during that tropical summer on the island that John suddenly felt the urge to compose music. At a dance club on the island he heard disco music in the hall above him. The music was by the punk rockers, B-52's shouting out "Rock Lobster." The sound struck him as the same type of music Yoko had wailed out a decade earlier. As he stood letting the sounds penetrate his creative mind, he even wondered if perhaps that punk rock group had taken their style from Yoko. Wherever the sound originated John had the dormant skills to enlarge upon it and make it "his and hers." He called Yoko in New York and over a period of a day they kept the lines open as they wrote, hummed, screamed and panted out their twenty or so songs that they decided to record as soon as they were together at the Record Plant in downtown New York. What they scribbled for lyrics in a "dyarriah" of activity, were words attached to music of what he and Yoko had experienced for the past five years living in seclusion.

Back in New York he and Yoko plunged into recording those recollections and released the new LP "Double Fantasy." Interestingly, the single from the album that made the charts fastest, was the catchy himily he titled, "Starting Over." Throughout the album of "Double Fantasy," the Lennons captured in verse their joy of life and living with each other. One of the songs, "Cleaning Up Time," tells of the pleasure of baking a loaf of bread; "Dear Yoko," is a love note; and "Watching the Wheels" tells the world that for John, it was fun at last merely to be a daydreaming spectator in life.

"We feel like this is just a start now," John commented to the radio interviewer the last afternoon of his life, "You see, 'Double Fantasy'—this is our first album. I know we've worked together before—but this is our first album. We feel, I feel, like nothing has ever happened before today!"

"I'm talking to guys and gals who had been through what we had been through together, the '60s group that has survived ... survived the war, the drugs, the politics, the violence on the street, the whole sha-bang."

What was it John had said? "And so good friend, you'll just have to carry on."

# 11

## He Made Us Happy

# 11

How ironical it was that the first word many heard about the death of John Lennon came from sports announcer, Howard Cosell in the heart of Monday night football when he interrupted his macho calling of the New England-Miami football game to say, "Ladies and gentlemen, we just received word that John Lennon of the Beatles was shot and killed in New York this evening."

He was called "another world citizen." His death had that type of effect.

"People are committing suicide," Yoko Ono said in a telephone call to the Daily News, the paper reported. "They are sending me telegrams saying that this is the end of an era and everything."

Comments came from all over the world:

"I am angry. I am trying to work harder so as not to cry in front of the mike. John belonged to us—all his fans."

"We were all indestructable. I remember speeding down a highway through a snowstorm with some friends, late at night; the car skidded and swerved, and suddenly we were crashing through a guardrail and the car was tumbling down a gully.

"When it came to a rest, we looked around at one another; there we were, in our high school letter jackets, unhurt, and the radio was still blaring and there were the Beatles singing 'I Want to Hold Your Hand.'

"And we stood in the snow, laughing; young and new and invincible, laughing."

"Everybody cared about him. He was what rock and roll was all about."

"They played in the best part of my life."

Many who mourned for John Lennon made reference to the legendary Elvis. In Memphis, two years before John's death, the motel signs were altered to express sympathy. It was expected that Elvis, the hometown-boy-made-good, would receive special treatment. But who would have guessed New York City with all its sophistication would pour 100,000 people into Central Park to pay their deepest respects? Or that in Sidney, Australia, thousands would march, and cluster to be near to someone who understood. It was repeated everywhere—San Francisco, London and Moscow. They were peaceful demonstrations of affection for one so much a part of their own life. The mood was much like mourning a member of one's family.

Now there was just the two of them, Yoko and Sean. They were more lonely than ever because each shared in their deepest affection a common object that was no more with them. How hard it must have been for Yoko to explain to Sean what had happened.

"I told Sean what happened. I showed him the picture of his father on the cover of the paper and explained the situation. I took Sean to the spot where John lay after he was shot. Sean wanted to know why the person shot John if he liked John. I explained that he was probably a confused person. Sean said we should find out if he was confused or if he really had meant to kill John. I said that was up to the court. He asked what court—a tennis court or a basketball court? That's how Sean used to talk with his father. They were buddies. John would have been proud of Sean if he had heard this. Sean cried later. He also said, 'Now Daddy is part of God. I guess when you die you become much more bigger because you're part of everything.'

"I don't have much more to add to Sean's statement. The silent vigil will take place December 14th at 2 p.m. for ten minutes.

"Our thoughts will be with you."

In a record shop in Westwood a young man in his late 20s spoke in a half-sigh. "Well," he said, "I guess now it's time to grow up," He spoke for an entire generation.

"It was a memorial for an age ... the '60s, when so much seemed possible," said freelance writer, Sarah Browning. "Lennon's death seals off that age forever."

"In Melbourne, Australia, several thousand people poured into the city square at 6 a.m. Monday local time—simultaneous with 2 p.m. New York time—to watch a giant video screen showing a Beatles concert."

"More than 500 North American radio stations played nothing but Lennon music yesterday or all weekend, and some observed the 10 minutes of silence that Ono had suggested as a tribute to the slain star. In Boston, WBCN-FM filled the ten minutes with 'environmental music,' sounds of waves, trees, birds, and rivers. Program director Tony Berardini said he felt that would honor Ono's wishes 'because it's nothing but natural silence.'"

In John Lennon's home town of Liverpool, England, a memorial concert turned into a near riot when nearly 30,000 fans mourning John's death swarmed over a makeshift stage when a band stopped playing Beatles music and strumbed up its own. Three persons were hospitalized before organizers switched on Beatle music from taped music piped into large outdoor speakers.

In Los Angeles, at the vigil for Lennon, a female guitarist dressed in black boots, struck up John's "Give Peace a Chance." Hundreds stood in a circle, hand in hand, and joined in singing what had become almost an anthem. The song rose and many who had not yet openly wept did as the words formed on their lips: "All we are saying is give peace a chance...."

KMET, "the station that rocks all of Southern California," observed an unprecedented ten-minute silence. The silence was appropriate to John's statement to Wayne "Tex" Barrett, when Lennon commented on death: "Death is only a dream."

The whole world of sensitive people who knew and understood John Lennon will miss him greatly. What more can be said?

# The 40 Years of John Lennon

## A Chronology

# A Chronology

## 1940

**October 9—Liverpool, England**
John Winston Lennon makes his first public appearance, his birth at Oxford Street Maternity Hospital

## 1955

**Liverpool**
John formed the Quarrymen, a musical group comprised of students from Quarrybank Grammar School

**June 15—Liverpool**
John meets Paul McCartney at a church social and Paul joins the Quarrymen.

## 1958

**July 15—Liverpool**
Julia Lennon, John's mother, dies when hit by a drunk driver while waiting at a bus stop

**August 29**
George Harrison joins the Quarrymen. The Quarrymen later change their name to Johnny and the Moondogs.

## 1959

Johnny and the Moondogs become the Silver Beatles

## 1961

**March 21—Liverpool**
Debut of The Beatles at the Cavern

**November 9—Liverpool**
Brian Epstein sees the Beatles perform at the Cavern

**December—Liverpool**
The Beatles sign their first contract with Brian Epstein.

## 1962

**January—Hamburg, Germany**
The Beatles open the Star Club in this city.

**August 1—Liverpool, England**
Ringo Starr joins the Beatles

The Beatles are now John on rhythm guitar (harmonica, organ, piano), Paul on bass (organ, piano, quitar), George on lead guitar and Ringo on drums.

**August 23—Liverpool**
John marries Cynthia Powell. Paul McCartney was his best man.

**September—London**
Beatles signed a contract with George Martin and record "Love Me Do" and "P.S. I Love You"—first single

**October 1—England**
Epsteins second contract. He is appointed manager for five years.

**November 26—England**
2nd single—"Please Please Me"

# 1963

**February 2—England**
The Beatles began their first British nationwide tour.

**February 19—England**
"Please Please Me" became the Beatles first song to become a #1 hit single in England.

**February 26—England**
Northern Songs Ltd. was formed with John Lennon, Paul McCartney, Brian Epstein and Dick James as its directors. Their first published song was "From Me To You."

**April 8—Sefton General Hospital, Liverpool**
John's first son is born and named John Charles Julian Lennon.

**April 12—England**
3rd single—"From Me To You" and "Thank You Girl"

**July 26—England**
*The Beatles* (No. 1) released in Britain; 100,000 advance orders awaited its release.

**August—Liverpool**
The Beatles' last appearance at the Cavern
4th single—"She Loves You" and "I'll Get You"

**October**
First gold record—"She Loves You"

**October 13—London**
Could this be the start of Beatlemania? The Beatles appear on *Sunday Night at the London Palladium* while overzealous fans riot outside.

**November 4—London**
The Beatles appear before the Queen Mother, Princess Margaret and Lord Snowden in the Royal Variety Show

**November 22—England**
*With the Beatles*, second LP released; 300,000 advance sales.

**November 30—England**
5th single—"I Want To Hold Your Hand" and "This Boy" One-half million advance order awaited its release.

### December—London
John and Paul are credited by the *Times* of London as being outstanding English composers of 1963.

### December 29—New York City
WMCA broadcasts the first Beatle song in the United States ("I Want To Hold Your Hand")

## 1964

### January 3—United States
Jack Paar Show clips of Beatles' concerts

### January
Capitol released first Beatles record in U.S.—"I Want To Hold Your Hand" and "I Saw Her Standing There." By mid-January, it had hit #1 in Australia.

### February 7—New York
Thousands of fans greet Beatles on their arrival at Kennedy Airport in New York. Riots took place outside their hotel.

### February 9—New York
Appeared on the Ed Sullivan Show; performed five numbers

### February 11—Washington
First live concert of the Beatles in the U.S. held at Washington Colliseum

### February 12—New York
Two sell-out performances at Carnegie Hall

### February 16—New York
Second appearance on the Ed Sullivan Show

**February 21—England**
Variety Club of Great Britain votes Beatles show business personalities of the year

**March 2—Liverpool**
Beatles began work on first film "A Hard Day's Night"

**March 13—United States**
*Meet the Beatles* sold over 3.5 million copies in the U.S. thus making it the best selling LP of all time.

**March 20—England**
6th single—"Can't Buy Me Love" and "You Can't Do That"

**March 23—England**
John published first book—*John Lennon In His Own Write*

**June 6—Amsterdam**
Beatles held a live concert in Amsterdam. Many tens of thousands crowded the streets.

**June 12—Australia**
An Australian tour begins with one-quarter of a million fans lining the streets of Melbourne

**July 6—London**
*A Hard Day's Night* film premiere at the London Pavillion

**July 10—England**
Single #7—"A Hard Day's Night" and "Things We Said Today"

**July 12—New York**
Film clips of *A Hard Day's Night* appear on Ed Sullivan's show

John Lennon purchases a home in Weybridge on St. George's Hill.

## July 29—Stockholm
John and Paul suffered severe electrical shocks while performing at a concert in Stockholm.

## August 12—United States
U.S. opening of *A Hard Day's Night*. More prints are made of this film than for any other film ever made.

## August 19—United States
The Beatles' second U.S. tour covering 18 states.

## September 11—Florida
Beatles refuse to play to a segregated audience in Jacksonville

## September 19—United States
John approves the printing of "The Fat Budgie," his cartoon drawing, as a Christmas card

## September 20—United States
Once again the Beatles appear on the Ed Sullivan Show

## September 25—England
A syndicate of American businessmen try to buy Brian Epstein's interest in the Beatles for 3.5 million pounds sterling. He refuses.

## October 16—England
Next single—"If I Fell" and "Tell Me Why"

## November 27—England
8th single—"I Feel Fine" and "She's A Woman"

**December 4—England**
LP *Beatles For Sale* released

**December 15—England**
*Beatles For Sale* sold almost 750,000 copies in two weeks.

# 1965

**January 9—England**
John Lennon read his poems on the BBC-2

**January 19—United States**
The Beatles receive four of the seven gold records awarded in the United States in 1964.

**February 11—England**
John and Cynthia attend Ringo Starr's marriage to Maureen Cox.

**Feburary 12—Bahamas**
The Beatles arrive to film "Help"

**April 9—England**
9th single—"Ticket to Ride" and "Yes It Is"

**May 12—Bahamas**
Film "Help" completed

**June 12—England**
Most Excellent Order of the British Empire (MBE) conferred on the Beatles. A furor ensued as some war heroes, former MBE awardees, sent their medals back in protest of the Beatles' being awarded the MBE.

**June—England**
John, promoting his second book, *A Spaniard in the Works*, appeared on BBC-TV's *Tonight*.

**June 24—Italy**
*A Spaniard in the Works* is published. John Lennon is interviewed on ITV's *Today*.

**June 24—Milan, Italy**
The Beatles' first Italian appearance opened to a sparce audience.

**July 23—England**
10th single—"Help!" and "I'm Down"

**July 29—England**
Princess Margaret and Lord Snowden attend the premier of "Help!"

**August 6—England**
John purchases a home, near Bournemouth, for the Aunt who raised him.

**August 15—United States**
Concert at Shea Stadium, New York. The Beatles captivate 56,000 people.

**August 24—England**
The Beatles' song publishing company, Northern Songs, reports profits of over 600,000 pounds sterling.

**September 12—United States**
Ed Sullivan Show appearance

**October 26—England**
The Queen of England bestows MBE on the Beatles at Buckingham Palace. John later admitted to being high on marijuana during the royal presentation.

**December 11—England**
11th single—"Day Tripper" and "We Can Work It Out"

## 1966

**February 4—United States**
Beatles receive three more U.S. gold records for "Help!" "Eight Days A Week," and "Yesterday."

**May 1—Britain**
Beatles appear for what will be their last live performance on stage in England at the annual *New Musical Express* poll winners concert.

**June 10—England**
12th single—"Paperback Writer" and "Rain"

**June 26—Germany**
Fans riot at two concerts given in Hamburg. Police were called in.

**June 30—Japan**
Two hundred thousand people applied for 10,000 seats in Tokyo for a Beatles concert.

**July 3—Manila**
Fifty thousand fans cheer the Beatles

**August**
Uproar caused over John Lennon's Christianity and Jesus remarks.

**August 4—United States**
Beatles records reported banned on radio stations in New York, Texas, Utah, and South Carolina.

**August 5—England**
13th single—"Yellow Submarine" and "Eleanor Rigby"

**August 6**
   Brian Epstein apologizes for the group as 30 American radio stations ban all Beatles records across the United States.

**August 11—United States**
   John Lennon apologizes when Beatles arrive in the U.S.

**August 12—United States**
   Third tour of the U.S. opens in Chicago. This would be their last U.S. concert tour.

**August 17—Toronto, Canada**
   John Lennon voices his approval of Americans avoiding the draft by fleeing to Canada.

**August 19—Memphis, Tennessee**
   Klu Klux Klan pickets a Beatles concert.

**August 23—New York**
   Shea Stadium concert was a sell out.

**August 28—Los Angeles, California**
   Beatles escape via armored car as the crowd riots.

**August 29—San Francisco, California**
   Candlestick Park is the site of the Beatles' final on stage performance together.

**September 1**
   *Action for the Crippled Child* receives a Christmas card design donated by John Lennon.

**September 19—Spain**
   John Lennon arrives to film "How I Won The War"

**November—London**
John meets Yoko Ono

**December 29**
Billboard reports 13 countries around the world show the Beatles at the top of the charts.

# 1967

**January 7—United States**
The Beatles receive six more gold records for 1966 hits.

**February 17—England**
14th single—"Penny Lane" and "Strawberry Fields Forever"

**March 11—United States**
For composing "Michelle," Lennon and McCartney receive the Grammy Award for Song of the Year.

**May 20—England**
"A Day in the Life" from *Sgt. Pepper's Lonley Hearts Club Band* is banned by the BBC as being condusive to encouraging drug abuse. The Beatles argued that it was not.

**May 27—England**
John announces that the band will no longer go on tour.

**June 25**
Our World, a TV program, shows the Beatles recording "All You Need is Love." Forty million people in 24 countries tune in.

**July 7—England**
15th single—"All You Need Is Love" and "Baby, You're a Rich Man"

**July 24—London**
The London *Times* ran a full page ad recommending the abolition of marijuana laws. The ad was signed by Brian Epstein, all four Beatles, plus other celebrities.

**August 27—England**
Brian Epstein found dead of an apparent drug overdose. The Beatles were with the Maharishi Mahesh Yogi in North Wales when they heard the news.

**August 31—England**
Beatles announce that they will manage themselves.

**September 11**
Work starts on the film "Magical Mystery Tour"

**September**
John and George Harrison, along with Maharishi Mahesh Yogi, appear on David Frost's show to discuss transcendental meditation.

**October 18**
*How I Won The War* film premiere

**November 24—England**
16th single—"Hello Goodbye" and "I Am the Walrus"

**December 26—England**
BBC shows *Magical Mystery Tour*. Critics pan it.

## 1968

**January 6—England**
Brian Epstein's fortune reported at 500,000 pounds sterling

**February—England**
Beatles form Apple Corporation Ltd.

**March, April—India**
Beatles, wives and entourage travel to India to study meditation with the Maharishi.

**March 9—United States**
*Sg. Pepper's Lonely Hearts Club Band*, the LP album, won Grammies for best album of the year, best contemporary album, best-engineered recording, and best album cover.

**March 15—England**
17th single—"Lady Madonna" and "The Inner Light"

**May—United States**
*Tonight* show is visited by John and Paul to promote Apple.

**May 22—United States**
John is quoted in an interview that the Vietnam War is "insane."

**June 15—England**
John and Yoko plant two acorns at Coventry Cathedral symbolizing the East-West accord he and Yoko had found.

**July 1**
John and Yoko announce their engagement. They release balloons to celebrate.

## July 13—England
Pandemonium broke out on Baker Street when all the stock of the Apple Boutique was given away to the crowds. Cost: 20,000 pounds sterling

## July 17—London
World premiere of *Yellow Submarine* film at London Pavillion draws Ringo and Marueen, Paul, and John and Yoko.

## August 11—England
Apple Records is launched as National Apple Week is declared.

## August 23—England
Reports are that Cynthia Lennon will sue John for divorce. Yoko Ono is listed as the reason.

## August 26—United States
18th single released—"Hey Jude" and "Revolution"

## September 8—London
Beatles appear on David Frost's *Frost on Sunday* show performing "Hey Jude."

## September 14
The Beatles' official biography was published. "Hey Jude" had already grossed 2 million copies.

## October 18—Marylebone, England
John and Yoko's apartment is raided by British police. They were both arrested for possession of marijuana and later that day released on bail.

**October 28—England**
Cynthia Lennon officially files for divorce.

**November 8—England**
While John and Yoko advertize in music journals for the "Peace Ship"—an independent radio station broadcasting peace messages to both sides in the Middle East, Cynthia Lennon receives her divorce.

**November 9—England**
Apple releases the LP "Unfinished Music No. 1—Two Virgins" by John and Yoko. Album cover shows them both nude.

**November 21—England**
Yoko Ono miscarries their baby. John remains by her side in the hospital.

**November 28—England**
John admitted possessing cannabis resin and was fined 150 pounds sterling by the courts. Yoko was not involved in the legal action.

**November 30**
"Hey Jude" sales reach six million worldwide

**December 18—London**
John and Yoko appear on stage at Albert Hall squirming in a large white bag

**December**
"Rape" was produced for Austrian TV by John and Yoko.
John and Yoko's Rock 'n' Roll Circus film was done but never released.

## 1969

**January 3—United States**
New Jersey officials seize thousands of the Two Virgin LPs as pornographic material

**January 30—London**
Last public Beatle concert held atop the Apple Building

**March 7—England**
John and Yoko gave a concert at Cambridge

**March 20—Gilbraltar**
While vacationing in Paris, John and Yoko took a day trip to Gibraltar and got married. Their witnesses were two Apple executives.

**March 21—England**
Allen Klein given a three-year contract to manage the Beatles and Apple.

**March 26—Holland**
John and Yoko demonstrate for peace by staging a "bed-in" at the Amsterdam Hilton where they were honeymooning.

**April 1—Vienna**
John and Yoko appear at a press conference the day following their premier of "Rape" espousing love and dressed in huge white pillow cases. Lennon stated that he was nearly broke and would go back to work recording with the Beatles.

**April 5—England**
ATV offers 9 million pounds sterling for Northern Songs.

**April 10—England**
John and Paul refuse to sell Northern Songs; instead offer to aquire ATV's 35%.

**April 18—England**
19th single—"Get Back" and "Don't Let Me Down"

**April 25—England**
Beatles offer 2.1 million pounds sterling for controlling interest in Northern Songs.

**April 26—England**
Atop the Apple building, during an official ceremony, John Winston Lennon changes his name to John Ono Lennon.

**May 1—England**
Apple released LP Unfinished Music No. 2—Life With the Lions by John and Yoko on their newly formed Zapple label.

**May 5—England**
John and Yoko reportedly purchase Tittenhurst Park, Ascot mansion with 72 acres of grounds

**May 20—England**
20th single—"The Ballad of John and Yoko" and "Old Brown Shoe"
This was the last single record that John and Paul worked on together.

**July 28—England and U.S.**
Apple releases the single of John Lennon and the Plastic Ono Band—"Give Peace a Chance" and "Remember Love"

## July—Scotland
John, Yoko and Kyoko (her daughter) were injured in a car accident.

## September—England
ATV reportedly purchased nearly 50% of Northern Songs trying to gain control.

## September 13—Toronto, Canada
Rock and Roll Revival Concert was held in Varsity Stadium by John and Yoko

## September—Britain
Apple releases "Abbey Road"

## October
John complains about the waste and mishandling of Apple's non-recording ventures—most of which were financial fiascos.

John and the Plastic Ono Band release "Cold Turkey" and "Don't Worry Kyoko," a single, through Apple.

## October 13—United States
21st single—"Something" and "Come Together"

## October 16—England
Beatles agree to sell to ATV all their shares in Northern Songs. Price to be arbitrated.

## November 25—England
As a protest against support of U.S. policy in Viet Nam and the British policy toward the Biafran War, John returned his MBE to Queen Elizabeth—with love

## 1970

**March 2—United States**
Apple releases John's single—"Instant Karma" and "Who Has Seen the Wind?"

**March 16—United States**
22nd single—"Let It Be" and "You Know My Name"

**April 10—England**
Derek Taylor, Apple's press officer, announces Paul McCartney's departure from the Beatles.

**May 14—New York**
Film *Let It Be* premiered in New York

**May 25th—United States**
23rd single—"The Long and Winding Road" and "For You Blue" Reportedly sold 1.2 million copies in two days.

**August 1**
An Italian hotel owner, Roberto Bassanini marries Cynthia Lennon

**September 22—United States**
Dick Cavett hosts John and Yoko on his show.

**September 28—England**
John and Paul jointly sue Northern Songs for one-half of all monies received

**December 31—England**
Legal proceedings were begun by Paul to end the business partnership of the Beatles.

# 1971

**January 4—England and United States**
Apple released John's next single "Mother" and "Why"

**February—England**
Paul's lawsuit is opposed in High Court by the other three Beatles, Allen Klein and Apple Corporation

**March 5—England**
John Lennon and the Plastic Ono Band release "Power to the People" and "Open Your Box"

**March 12—England**
A receiver is appointed by the High Court to handle the Beatles' assets. Allen Klein is not allowed, by the court, to have any further dealings in managing the group's affairs.

**March 19—England**
John, George, Ringo appeal the receivership.

**April 29—United States**
Single "Power to the People" and "Touch Me" released.

**May 15—Cannes, France**
Two of John and Yoko's films (Apotheosis and Fly) are featured at the Filmmaker's Fortnight Festival

**August—United States**
John and Yoko moved to New York City

**October 4—United States**
Single "Imagine" and "It's So Hard" released

**December 6—United States**
John releases single "Happy Xmas (War Is Over)" and "Listen, the Snow is Fallin."

# 1972

**January 13—United States**
John and Yoko again are guests of the David Frost Show.

**February 21-25—New York**
John and Yoko cohost the Mike Douglas Show.

**February 29—United States**
John's visa expires. He remains in the U.S. to search for Kyoko (Yoko's daughter). His battle with the immigration authorities begins as the U.S. government refuses to allow him to stay.

**April 4—United States**
Dick Cavett had John and Yoko on his show

**May 8—United States and England**
Single—John and Yoko release "Woman Is the Nigger Of the World" and "Sisters, O Sisters"

**May 11—England**
Once again John and Yoko appear on the Dick Cavett Show.

Yoko's exhibit at the Everson Museum became the basis for a TV Special entitled *John and Yoko in Syracuse, New York*

**August 31—Madison Square Garden, New York**
John and Yoko appear as headline entertainers at a benefit concert for the mentally retarded

**December 15—United States**
A film of the August 31st concert was shown on TV.

**December 23—United States**
*Imagine*, John and Yoko's new movie premieres.

## 1973

**March**
U.S. Immigration calls for John's deportation because of his drug conviction from 1968 in Britain

**July**
John, George and Ringo team up for one song, "I'm the Greatest" for the *Ringo* album. It was the first time they recorded together in four years.

**October—New York**
John and Yoko separated. John moved to Los Angeles.

**October 22**
John's single "Mind Games" and "Meat City" released.

## 1974

**February**
Beatles' receiver indicates a resolution of the financial dilemma should soon be reached. Legally, it appears they will be bound until 1976.

### July 26—Boston
A Beatles Appreciation Convention draws 2,000 fans who demonstrated against John's impending deportation. A similar event was held in New York a few months later.

### August 31—New York
John, in federal court, blames the Nixon Administration for trying to deport him because he had helped to organize the antiwar demonstration outside the Republican National Convention in 1972. He also claimed that his phone had been illegally tapped.

### September 23
Elton John played piano, organ and sang on John's next single "Whatever Gets You Thru the Night" and "Beef Jerky"

### November 28—New York
John Lennon and Elton John appear at Madison Square Garden together.

### Decemeber 16
Reports stated that Nixon, while President, had ordered the deportation and harassment of John Lennon.
John's single released—"No. 9 Dream" and "What You Got"

## 1975

### January 9—England
Court dissolves last legal ties of the Beatles.

### March 1—United States
Grammy awards show had John Lennon as a presenter.

**March 10—New York City**
Apple releases single—"Stand By Me" and "Move Over Ms. L"

**March—New York City**
John returns from Los Angeles and joins Yoko

**April 28—United States**
John is a guest on the Tomorrow show.

**May 21—United States**
David Frost airs The Beatles Special

**October 9—New York**
Sean Ono, a son, is born to John and Yoko after her having three previous miscarriages. The event happens on John's 35th birthday

## 1976

**May 31—United States**
Capitol releases single "Got to Get You into My Life" and "Helter Skelter"

**July 27—United States**
U.S. Government drops efforts to deport John and issues him a green card.

## 1977

**May—Japan**
John, Yoko and Sean visit the baby's grandparents

## 1978

**February 19**
T.V. Special

## 1979

**May 27**
Open letter from John and Yoko appears in the newspaper for their fans

## 1980

**July—**
While sailing from Newport, Rhode Island to Bermuda, John is caught in a storm while on a yacht. During his Bermuda vacation he becomes inspired and resumes his musical composing.

**October 9—New York**
John's 40th Birthday

**November**
"Double Fantasy" released by Lennon Music Inc., John's new company.

**December 6—New York**
Mark David Chapman arrives from Honolulu

**Decmeber 8—New York**
John Lennon is killed by four shots from Mark Chapman's gun.
Ironically, "Double Fantasy" had gone gold that day, topping the one million copies sold mark.

**December 14—Worldwide**
A 10-minute vigil is held worldwide to commemorate John Lennon's death.

# Sources

# Bibliography

# *Sources*

## Chapter 1
*Newsweek*, "Death of a Beatle," December 22, 1980.
*L.A. Times*, "Lennon: Beatle Shot to Death," December 9, 1980.
Combined Newspaper Accounts and Newsweek, December 1980.
*Newsweek*, "Strawberry Fields Forever," December 22, 1980.
*L.A. Times*, "New York Says Goodby to John Lennon," December 16, 1980.

## Chapter 2
*Philadelphia Daily News*, December 10, 1980.
*Review Journal*, December 10, 1980.
*Newsweek*, "George, Paul, Ringo and John," February 24, 1964.

## Chapter 3
*Look*, December 13, 1966.
*The Sunday Times*, "John Lennon," December 14, 1980.
*Sunday Mirror*, "John—by the Stars Who Love Him," December 14, 1980.
*Las Vegas Sun*, "Lennon's Last Interview," December 10, 1980.

*Esquire,* "John Rennon's Excrusive Groupie," December 1970.

## Chapter 4
*Time,* "The Last Day In the Life," December 22, 1980.
*The Beatles Illustrated Lyrics 2,* Delta/Seymour Lawrence.
*Look,* "Lennon for Real," December 13, 1966.

## Chapter 5
*Time,* "The Last Day In the Life," December 22, 1980.
*The Beatles Illustrated Lyrics 2,* Delta/Seymour Lawrence.
*Saturday Review,* "Danger—Beatles At Work," October 12, 1968.
*Sunday Mirror,* "John—by the Stars Who Loved Him," December 14, 1980.

## Chapter 6
*Barry Miles,* "Beatles In Their Own Words," Omnibus Press, 1976.
*New York Times,* "They Changed Rock," March 20, 1978.
*A Twist of Lennon,* Cynthia Lennon, Avon, 1978.

## Chapter 7
*The Beatles Illustrated Lyrics 2,* Delta/Seymour Lawrence.
*Nation,* "About the Awful," June 8, 1964.
*Esquire,* "John Rennon's Ecrusive Groupie," December 1970.
*L.A. Times,* "Beatlemania Reached Around the World," December 12, 1980.

## Chapter 8
*The Sunday Telegraph,* "Lennon Before the Fame," December 14, 1980.
*Saturday Review,* "John and Yoko Ono Lennon; Give Peace a Chance," June 28, 1969.

## Chapter 9
*Life,* "The Beatles Decide," April 24, 1970.
*Newsweek,* "The Beatles Minus One," April 20, 1970.
*National Review,* "Settling Down," February 9, 1971.
*Ramparts Magazine,* "Lennon: The Working Class Hero Turns Red," July, 1971.

## Chapter 10
*Commonweal,* "John Lennon Speaking," September 22, 1972.

*New Yorker*, "Lennon," February 27, 1971.
*New York Times*, "They Changed Rock," March 20, 1978.

## Chapter 11

*Las Vegas Review Journal*, "Lennon," December 11, 1980.
*Las Vegas Sun*, "Beatles Fans Stunned," December 10, 1980.
Letter issued to media by Yoko Ono Lennon, December 10, 1980.
*L.A. Times*, "The Day the Music Died," December 10, 1980.
*San Francisco Chronicle*, "Tearful Vigil For John Lennon," December 15, 1980.